"The power of the Word has always moved entire cultures and societies. The gospel is the greatest incorporation of that power. In *Going Public with the Gospel*, Lon and Mark are simply stating a truth that our culture and our world needs. They know that as truth is proclaimed, it will never come back void, but will literally change souls."

TOM PHILLIPS, VICE PRESIDENT OF TRAINING, BILLY GRAHAM
EVANGELISTIC ASSOCIATION, AND EXECUTIVE DIRECTOR,
BILLY GRAHAM TRAINING CENTER

"I believe that this is a book that many of us have been awaiting for a long time. And Lon Allison and Mark Anderson are uniquely qualified to write it. Those who believe in public evangelism will be encouraged and better equipped to enable it. For those who have believed that the day for mass evangelism has passed, this book can revolutionize their thinking and their involvement in sharing the gospel with lost people of every generation."

PAUL CEDAR, CHAIRMAN, MISSION AMERICA COALITION

"This is one of the most important books I've read on proclamation evangelism. *Going Public with the Gospel* is an unusually readable book with an urgent message. Drawing upon Scripture, history and their own extensive experience, Allison and Anderson have written a book that should be required reading for evangelists, pastors, educators, parachurch leaders and every person preparing for Christian ministry."

LYLE W. DORSETT, PROFESSOR OF EVANGELISM AND SPIRITUAL
FORMATION, WHEATON COLLEGE AND GRADUATE SCHOOL

"This is a bold and provocative book. Against the conventional wisdom that mass evangelism is through, it asserts the ongoing priority of evangelistic preaching. Against the comfortable marketing mentality of much contemporary outreach, it calls for costly grace and radical discipleship. Against much timidity about supernatural acts it dares to say the Spirit is alive and well! You may not agree with all the authors propose to be challenged. It may shake our complacency. It may also, God willing, help to raise up a new generation of evangelists with the fire of God in their tongues, their heads and their bellies."

LEIGHTON FORD, PRESIDENT, LEIGHTON FORD MINISTRIES

"Lon Allison and Mark Anderson make a convincing case for evangelistic preaching. More to the point, they tell how to do it. Full of refreshing insights and contemporary applications."

ROBERT E. COLEMAN, DISTINGUISHED PROFESSOR OF EVANGELISM AND DISCIPLESHIP, GORDON-CONWELL THEOLOGICAL SEMINARY

"*Going Public with the Gospel* gives fresh legs to the Pauline question, how can people find and develop faith without evangelistic preaching? It compellingly confronts the erroneous assumption that today's sound-bite generation rejects the God-ordained means for proclaiming the good news. This is an important book by practitioners whose perspective comes from time-tested experience."

PAUL D. ROBBINS, PRESIDENT, CHRISTIANITY TODAY INTERNATIONAL

"Is public proclamation of the gospel still important? Many argue that with the rise of postmodernism the end of evangelistic preaching is near. Before you bury the tried and true method of gospel preaching you should first weigh this well-written clarion call for proclamation powerfully linked with the incarnational witness of the church."

JOHN H. ARMSTRONG, PRESIDENT, REFORMATION & REVIVAL MINISTRIES

"*Going Public with the Gospel* is a 'home run' that touches all the bases of proclamation evangelism. My good friends Lon Allison and Mark Anderson bring two unique perspectives to bear on this vital but sometimes overlooked aspect of ministry. A must-read for anyone who is interested in changing lives through evangelism."

STEVE WINGFIELD, FOUNDER, PRESIDENT AND EVANGELIST, WINGFIELD MINISTRIES

"A valuable, insightful and thought-provoking book. A 'must' book for every preacher."

J. JOHN, EVANGELIST, AUTHOR AND FOUNDER OF THE PHILO TRUST

"A challenging and engaging (evangelistic) call to arms. The inner section of evangelism and preaching is at the heart of the New Testament, here its huge implications for our day are fleshed out. I found the section on the content of gospel preaching especially sobering, the one on the power of God unusually uplifting."

ROB BUGH, SENIOR PASTOR, WHEATON BIBLE CHURCH,
WHEATON, ILLINOIS

"In this book Allison and Anderson provide an important reminder that the oft-maligned evangelistic preaching is still a powerful and effective method for gospel proclamation."

JOHN E. PHELAN JR., PRESIDENT AND DEAN,
NORTH PARK THEOLOGICAL SEMINARY

"Lon Allison and Mark Anderson's combined decades of 'in the trench' experience in evangelism around the world make them uniquely qualified to challenge the global church to better utilize the gift of the evangelist, a calling so woefully underutilized in many parts of the world today. Their ability to combine passion for the subject with positive ways forward makes this book worth reading for anyone with a heart to see God's kingdom advanced in our generation."

KEVIN PALAU, EXECUTIVE VICE PRESIDENT,
LUIS PALAU EVANGELISTIC ASSOCIATION

"*Going Public with the Gospel* communicates in a way that will force you to rethink ideas that you have never questioned before about proclamation evangelism. May it serve as a great encouragement to call out many new voices to proclaim the good news and re-ignite the pilot light of evangelistic preaching in our desperate world."

CARSON N. PUE, PRESIDENT, ARROW LEADERSHIP MINISTRIES,
VANCOUVER, BRITISH COLUMBIA

"In a world where so many say the role of faith in our lives should be private, bravo for two friends who challenge us to make it public! Resourced by an enormously effective career history of proclaiming Christ in the most innovative ways possible, Lon and Mark illuminate the way forward for proclamation of the good news. It is a must-read for anyone wanting to live seriously the Great Commission of Jesus. The stories, hope and tools in these pages give me courage and insight for a life of bold witness, and their challenge comes at a critical time for our world."

LORNA DUECK, EVANGELIST, JOURNALIST,
THE GLOBE AND MAIL

"Are my words getting through? Are they making a difference? In a world with hundreds of competing voices and thousands of high-tech distractions vying for the attention of our hearers, we have good reason to wonder. What a shot in the arm this book is! Grounded in solid thinking and filled with real-world examples, *Going Public with the Gospel* is a rich reminder of God's delight in using the simple spoken word. Lon and Mark bolstered my confidence, offered many practical suggestions and reinvigorated me for the task."

DAVID HENDERSON, SENIOR PASTOR, COVENANT PRESBYTERIAN CHURCH, WEST LAFAYETTE, INDIANA, AUTHOR OF *CULTURE SHIFT: COMMUNICATING GOD'S TRUTH TO OUR CHANGING WORLD*

"This book is long overdue! Anderson and Allison remind us of the tremendous power of the gospel message as they urge us not to neglect its public proclamation. Their insight on the content required to preach the gospel biblically and their challenge not to neglect communicating the whole gospel—particularly the uncomfortable parts—is desperately needed in our self-focused age. Their stories are moving; their styles of communicating Christ are creative and inspiring. This book is not just for those gifted to proclaim Christ publicly; it will help anyone who longs to communicate the gospel with passion, fire and accuracy."

REBECCA MANLEY PIPPERT, EVANGELIST, AUTHOR OF *OUT OF THE SALTSHAKER*

GOING PUBLIC
WITH THE GOSPEL

REVIVING EVANGELISTIC PROCLAMATION

Lon Allison and Mark Anderson

InterVarsity Press
Downers Grove, Illinois

InterVarsity Press
P.O. Box 1400, Downers Grove, IL 60515-1426
World Wide Web: www.ivpress.com
E-mail: mail@ivpress.com

InterVarsity Press® is the book-publishing division of InterVarsity Christian Fellowship/USA®, a student
movement active on campus at hundreds of universities, colleges and schools of nursing in the United States
of America, and a member movement of the International Fellowship of Evangelical Students. For information
about local and regional activities, write Public Relations Dept., InterVarsity Christian Fellowship/USA, 6400
Schroeder Rd., P.O. Box 7895, Madison, WI 53707-7895, or visit the IVCF website at <www.ivcf.org>.

All Scripture quotations, unless otherwise indicated, are taken from the Holy Bible, New International
Version®. NIV®. Copyright ©1973, 1978, 1984 by International Bible Society. Used by permission of
Zondervan Publishing House. All rights reserved.

Design: Cindy Kiple

Images: Mike Powell and Hulton Archive/Getty Images

Appendix material from Dallas Anderson and Gary Cobb is used with permission.

ISBN 0-8308-1365-9

Printed in the United States of America ∞

Library of Congress Cataloging-in-Publication Data

Allison, Lon (Lon J.), 1952-
    Going public with the Gospel: reviving evangelistic proclamation/
Lon Allison and Mark Anderson.
        p. cm.
Includes bibliographical references.
    ISBN 0-8308-1365-9 (pbk.: alk. paper)
1. Evangelistic work. I. Anderson, Mark (Mark E.), 1957-   II. Title.
BV3790.A49 2004
251'.3—dc22

                                                                    2003018831

P	17	16	15	14	13	12	11	10	9	8	7	6	5	4	3	2	1
Y	15	14	13	12	11	10	09	08	07	06	05	04	03				

CONTENTS

Acknowledgments 8

Introduction 9

  1 The Power of Speech 17

PART 1: THE WONDER OF PUBLIC PROCLAMATION

  2 The Power of Public Proclamation 29

  3 Biblical Foundations of Public Proclamation 38

  4 The History of Public Proclamation 50

PART 2: WHAT HAPPENED TO EVANGELISTIC PREACHING?

  5 The Case of the Missing Evangelist 71

  6 The Lost Gospel 85

PART 3: LET'S GO! TAKING IT TO THE STREETS

  7 Preaching Christ 99

  8 Seeking Relevance 112

  9 The Demonstration of Truth 124

  10 Spiritual Warfare 138

  11 Preservation 147

Epilogue: *Faith and Vision—Who Will Hear and Believe?* 161

Appendix 1: *Rationale and Suggestions for Using the*
          Five Points in Presenting the Gospel 171
          Dallas Anderson

Appendix 2: *An Overview of Follow-Up* 176
          Gary Cobb

Notes 179

ACKNOWLEDGMENTS

To Karen, my wife and best friend. You've been my soulmate since we were teenagers. Your godly example as a wife, mother and partner in ministry has helped shape what I believe.

To our six children, you are all amazing gifts from God. Your love toward the Lord brings great joy to my life.

To Barb, my assistant, who for many years has dealt with my quirks, offering valuable and much-needed insight along the way.

Loren Cunningham, who opened the door for me into YWAM, allowing me room to fulfill my God-given vision.

My friend and coauthor Lon, who helps me balance some of my radical perspectives.

Mark Anderson

To my lovely and gifted wife, Marie. You are a better evangelist than me. Your heart for the lost and devotion to the local church keep me on track.

To Tara, Courtney and Eric, our children in the Lord. You keep me sane. I love you.

To Jim Persson and Leighton Ford, who each taught me by instruction and example that the chief purpose of life is to glorify God by bearing much fruit.

And finally to coauthor and friend Mark. You are a wild man. Keep it up.

Lon Allison

INTRODUCTION

But I wish to say most emphatically that where a speaker has that gift,
the direct evangelical appeal of the "Come to Jesus" type
can be as overwhelming today as it was a hundred years ago.
I have seen it done, preluded by a religious film and
accompanied by hymn singing, and with remarkable effect.
I cannot do it; but those who can ought to do it with all their might.

C. S. LEWIS, *GOD IN THE DOCK*

Whenever we read a book or listen to a speaker or teacher, we find ourselves wondering about the communicator's life journey. So, to begin our book, we want to tell you a bit of our stories, especially as they relate to our theme.

LON ALLISON'S JOURNEY ON THE THEME

I didn't grow up in a Christian home, though I'm endlessly grateful for a loving father and mother, still together after fifty years. Ours was a good, moral home, but there was very little religious life. I remember the first time I went to church at age ten. What a shock! The building was different from any store or house I'd been in. The music didn't sound like the Beach Boys or Peter, Paul & Mary. And when the leader stood to speak, he wore a long, black dress—strangest thing I'd ever seen. I didn't understand him, his words or the book he read from on that Easter morning. If God lived there, he was from another planet.

A couple of years later, we needed the men in the black dresses. Disaster hit our suburban California life when my little brother drowned in our swimming pool. The church building, with its long wooden pews and filtered light from the colored window glass, seemed a strange place to say goodbye to Stevie. But the men in black dresses read from the book and said words that helped a bit. They were words about God and Jesus, his Son, and heaven and hope. I was thirteen, and it was my first exposure to gospel speech, but it started its work in my life.

In my eleventh-grade year, a friend finally convinced me to attend a "youth group." I'd been saying no for two years, but this time her invitation included the news that the girl I liked was in the group. I went, I saw, I conquered. She became my girlfriend. But far more important, every Tuesday night we'd attend the group together. It was a Young Life club, and it was quite different from the place of pews, filtered light and strange music. It was fun and it was interesting. I remember being surprised that the person who talked read from the same book, the Bible, but didn't wear a black dress. He spoke about God and Jesus, and he talked about our lives. His name was Bob Lonac, and he will always have an important place in my life because he started my journey toward the new life I didn't even know existed.

At first I didn't listen very much, because I had the girl and a '57 Chevy, and we won the league in football. But when the girl broke up with me for another guy, my world fell apart. Now on Tuesdays I began to listen—hard. Bob made Jesus seem like he was across the room. I began to visualize what Jesus looked like. I was amazed by the things he did. I was hit hard by the real story of the cross. I hadn't realized it hurt Jesus that much. Every week the gospel was told one piece at a time. Most of all, I learned that this Jesus promised to never leave or forsake me (see Heb 13:5).

God was putting the pieces together. It took time. Sin meant my badness was a problem not only for me but also for God. The cross was for me as much as for the whole world. The resurrection meant he was really powerful, and even more, real and alive today. Finally one night when I was alone in my bed, God brought the Jesus stories all together, and in my simple, quite incomplete and totally selfish way, I asked Jesus to come into my life. I wanted someone who wouldn't leave or forsake me.

Throughout the rest of that year, I listened to many more Jesus talks. I read the Book and some other books too, but it was only when the ideas were presented through the speech of real and honest people that it made sense. I went to a summer camp where for six straight nights another speaker without a black dress filled in the stories from his perspective. I would go out to the dock of the Malibu Club in Canada and talk with God afterward while the waters of the inlet lapped quietly on the pylons. I'd found Jesus (actually he'd found me), and he was with me forever, or so the Book and the speakers said.

I didn't know my life would also be given to speaking Jesus' story. I started as a raw recruit, learning by watching others, listening to their words and catching ideas from their style. I was diverted for a time, spending a good part of a decade learning to utilize my body and my emotions, as well as my mind, as a professional actor. For a while I thought Shakespeare would end up as my book of stories. But soon I realized that, while doing Shakespeare was a privilege, proclaiming Jesus was a compulsion. His story brings all the stories of life together.

Even as I sit now writing these thoughts, overlooking the same inlet at that Malibu camp thirty-three years later, I'm a bit stunned. This time I'm the Jesus storyteller, and I still tremble each time I pick up this awesome mantle. With his guidance and courage, I've spoken the Story thousands of times to tens of thousands of people at camps, in local churches, in movie theaters, in outdoor arenas, in Laundromats, in clubhouses, in civic centers and on the backs of pickup trucks. I've spoken the Story to kids and children, to farmers and CEOs, and through translators in a few lands. I've spoken in blue jeans, suits, khakis and Birkenstocks. I've even gladly worn the black dress a few times. The Story is the great story, for every people in every time. And when it is told through men and women yielded to Christ who love their listeners, it does the impossible—bringing salvation to formally lost people—for "God was pleased through the foolishness of what was preached to save those who believe" (1 Cor 1:21).

MARK ANDERSON'S JOURNEY ON THE THEME

It was a hot night in July 1973. A friend told me that there was something special going on each night at the Minnesota State Fairgrounds in St. Paul.

When we got there, we found out that it was a Billy Graham mission. As I sat in the sweltering heat and listened to Graham's message, I noticed that something was different about him. He sounded like he knew Jesus—much like my great-grandfather, a preacher and church planter.

At the end of the service, I really wanted to join the crowds thronging to the front, but I held on to the chair in front of me. At last, Graham said, "This is the final call. If you are coming to give your heart to Jesus tonight, you must step out right now and make your way down front." Almost before I realized it, I moved out and joined the flood of seekers streaming down the aisles. The prayer I prayed that night changed my life forever.

Immediately I felt a deep passion for the lost. I told everybody I met about Jesus and how my life had been changed. One of the most meaningful of these conversations was when I prayed with my father, who had struggled with alcohol for some time. My heart welled with joy as I watched old things pass away and all things become new (see 2 Cor 5:17). He was delivered instantaneously from his craving for alcohol and has served the Lord for more than twenty-five years.

After I had "practiced" on my family and friends for several years, the Lord opened the door for me to go into full-time evangelism, working with Lowell Lundstrom Ministries as a campaign coordinator. These early days were fun and full of adventure. My wife, Karen, and I were newly married and traveling with two young children.

In 1983 a good friend and I planted a church in Minneapolis. Ted Lyke was pastoral, and I was more evangelistic in nature. Our giftings fit together well. During those pastoring years I founded an international ministry called Church on the Move. It was here I began to develop evangelism strategies and to take the gospel to the nations of the world. This ministry focused on church planting combined with social work. We established Christian schools, medical clinics and literacy centers through our campaigns.

In 1989 I met Loren Cunningham, the founder of Youth With A Mission (YWAM). This relationship helped take my views on evangelism and world missions to a whole new level. In 1992 I formally joined YWAM and began campaigns as an evangelistic arm of the organization. What has happened since is beyond even my biggest dreams as a youth. God is allowing us to reach people all over the earth through more than one hundred citywide campaigns a year.

Karen, my wife since we were nineteen, has been an integral part of the ministry. We now have six children who love Jesus and who are focused on reaching out to the lost. Our oldest daughter, Christelle, and her husband, Antonio, serve on staff with me in ministry. Our second-oldest daughter, Lindsay, and her husband, Sean, are focused on using their college educations to make a difference for Christ in the private sector. Our younger children are already discussing their futures in ministry and missions.

It all started at the fairgrounds in St. Paul on that hot July night in 1973. I am eternally grateful that Graham paid the price to obey the command of Jesus to "go and preach." Today, when I watch hundreds of people—especially youth—streaming down the aisles at our campaigns, I'm reminded of that life-changing early decision.

Thank God for the ministry of the evangelist!

THE PURPOSE OF THIS BOOK

This book is written for two reasons. First, we want to convince the kingdom church that the proclamation of the gospel is a vital and primary means to lead the lost world to Christ. Going public with the gospel is a divinely ordained method. It always has been. If you're not convinced of that, we pray you will be by the time we conclude. We believe speech has the power to persuade. We believe public speech has the power not only to persuade individuals but also to bring about the transformation of societies. We also will argue that public proclamation of the gospel is a vital component of spiritual warfare. Therefore, to a Western church that quickly runs to any and every "new" method to reach the world, we simply say, "There is nothing quite as powerful and effective as proclaiming Christ in the public square."

Not many books of recent years focus on public proclamation as a key strategy for evangelism. Books on personal evangelism abound. The church is indebted to titles such as *Becoming a Contagious Christian*, *Out of the Saltshaker* and *Living Proof*, just to name a few. Other authors have focused on church-growth principles to help transform churches into evangelizing agencies. Thom Rainer's *Surprising Insights from the Unchurched and Proven Ways to Reach Them* and Rick Warren's *The Purpose-Driven Church* are tremendous contributions. Still others offer encouragement for specific strategies, such as the Alpha Course and Compassion Evangelism, or even the tried and true Evangelism Explosion. These and many, many others are wonderful helps in evangelism. But there has been a dearth of writing on the subject of public proclamation evangelism. We seek to redress this issue.

Please understand that we believe proclamation evangelism is but one link in the chain, one step in the process of faith for lost people. The journey to Christ is different for every person, but one thing is clear: it is a journey. Public proclamation evangelism is generally seen as the step when an investigating person crosses the line to believing faith. This is true. However, it also assists those not ready to cross the line by providing a next step.

Public proclamation evangelism works in various settings. We tend to think of it in large-group settings (for instance, a Graham mission or festival). Many of our examples focus on multiple-church or area-wide settings, primarily because Mark leads an international campaign organization. However, public proclamation is just as effective in local church, conference or affinity-group settings. The values and effects are identical regardless of the setting, as long as the hard work of preparation and preservation are pursued.

Second, we want to propose some effective ways to proclaim Christ publicly in the present world. The gospel has not changed, but the world is always changing, whether you see it through cultural or through philosophical lenses. Therefore "ways and means" is an important topic to address. We will share stories from a variety of places and from many different evangelism-centered agencies displaying effective gospel proclamation. We'll even look at the past to find historical examples of public proclamation that have dramatically impacted nations. Intertwined with these stories from the present and the past are key principles that we can prayerfully employ today.

Keep in mind that when we speak of a nation, at times we are referring to a geographical area, but more often we will use the term as Scripture does. Jesus used the word *ethnos*, meaning a people or cultural group. The New Testament clearly demonstrates that evangelism is most effective when tailored to fit each cultural context. Therefore gospel speech, or public gospel proclamation, must be carefully and sensitively delivered in the context of the culture we address.

Jesus and his disciples practiced public gospel proclamation. But with proclamation, they added the demonstration of the truth they proclaimed. As they preached publicly, they combined it with acts of compassion and justice and the ministries of signs and wonders—and the church was established in the first century. It has advanced in the same ways over the last two millennia.

Scripture exhorts us not to forget this. At the end of his ministry life on earth, Jesus said, "Go into all the world and preach the good news to all creation. . . . And these signs will accompany those who believe" (Mk 16:15, 17). The response of the disciples was to go out and preach everywhere, and the Lord worked with them and confirmed his word by signs that accompanied it. The pattern is still the same, though the methods must continually change to remain relevant to an ever-changing world.

It is our hope that while reading this book you'll be reawakened to the desperate need to proclaim Christ publicly to today's world. There has never been a more important time for public proclaimers to stand up, be emboldened and proclaim the truth with Christ's compassion as our hallmark.

The sword of the Spirit, which is the Word of God, is the weapon that God has given to us to use offensively. We dream of seeing the gospel preached to every person, every nation and every generation, and we seek this in our lifetimes!

1

THE POWER OF SPEECH

I (Lon) remember the first time a speech shook me. I was on a date with a young woman from my high school. I chose a movie that would, I was told, put romance in the air. It was the late 1960s, and the movie was *Camelot*. I fully intended to endure the film, hoping to please the young lady, but I wasn't ready for the likes of King Arthur.

In a climactic moment, King Arthur faces a horrendous decision. He discovers that his queen and beloved, Guinevere, has betrayed him with his best friend and warrior, Lancelot. Standing alone in the dim light of the throne room, taking the sword Excalibur in his hand, Arthur speaks to himself a riveting monologue. In but a few hundred words, the choices between love and revenge, civilization and anarchy, are dissected. Will Arthur take revenge, or follow the painful path of love, allowing his own soul to be crushed? Will he be a man or a king? As the king, he must execute judgment on wrongdoing. As a man, and a noble one, he can choose love and forgiveness. Huge concepts and shattering ideas are spoken in but a few sentences.

At that time, I didn't know much about Jesus Christ. His words and life were new to me. But in Arthur, I heard the echo of Christ. Like Arthur, Jesus was a king who could rightly bring judgment. As the Son of Man, he would choose the fateful path of love. It killed him and, like Arthur, his earthly kingdom appeared lost. In Arthur's speech, I was hearing the shadow of God's eternal gospel.

I don't remember anything else about that night. In fact, I don't even remember which girlfriend I escorted to the film. But I remember Arthur's monologue. Oh, the power of words well conceived and spoken. They are alive. They can shape values and form our worldviews. They can even, as we will show, bring eternal salvation. But before we start talking about the special form of speech we call gospel proclamation, let's consider another example of speech's power to persuade.

A CLASH OF TITANS

Most historians would say the war in Europe began in 1939 when Germany invaded Poland. That is when the German army fired the first shots, but the war actually began years earlier. This war was a war of words, of ideas presented in speech and rhetoric so persuasive that millions of Germans rallied around the man Adolf Hitler. In 1938 he had convinced millions of followers of the rightness of the German cause.

> If at times today in foreign countries, parliamentarians or politicians venture to maintain that Germany has not kept her treaties, we can remind them of the greatest breach of a treaty that was ever practiced on the German people. Every promise which had been made to Germany in the Fourteen Points [after WWI]—those promises on the faith of which Germany had laid down her arms—was afterward broken. In 1932 Germany faced final collapse. The German Reich and people both seemed lost. And then came the German resurrection.[1]

Three years later, with the world at war, Hitler rallied the German people with further persuasive eloquence:

> I place my confidence in the best army in the world, in the best army which the German nation has ever possessed. It is numerically strong, it has the finest weapons and is better led than ever before. . . . Wherever we look today, we see a bodyguard of chosen men to whom the German soldiers have been entrusted. Behind these soldiers and their leaders stands the German nation, the whole German people. . . . I look to the future with fanatical confidence. The whole nation has

answered the call. I know that when the command is given: Forward march! Germany will march.[2]

To be sure, Hitler's rhetoric was born of the cultural situation in which the German people lived. Hitler read his culture, exegeted it the way an actor studies the content of a play, the way a preacher mines a passage looking for nuggets of biblical truth. The truth was, the German people had felt unjustly treated by western Europe ever since the conclusion of World War I. Harsh economic realities only exacerbated their frustrations. In other words, they were primed for the Hitler "magic."

Great Britain entered the war on September 3, 1939. The battle of words, however, was enjoined in earnest on May 13, 1940, by the warrior of words: Winston Churchill. The occasion was his election as prime minister. As Parliament convened, he gave his now famous pronouncement: "I have nothing to offer but blood, toil, tears and sweat." Three weeks later, on June 4, Churchill's greatest missile was launched. Before the House of Commons and live over the BBC, the Lion of England roared:

> Victory at all costs, victory in spite of all terror; victory however long and hard the road may be; for without victory there will be no survival. ... We shall not flag or fail. We shall go on to the end. We shall fight in France, we shall fight on the seas and the oceans, we shall fight with growing confidence and growing strength in the air, we shall defend our island, whatever the cost shall be, we shall fight on the beaches, we shall fight on the landing grounds, we shall fight in the fields, and in the streets, we shall fight in the hills, we shall never surrender![3]

The effect and power of Churchill's words was amazing. From that speech, the people of Great Britain rallied with new sustaining hope. Across the Atlantic an American president listened. Roosevelt was persuaded by Churchill's words and decided the United States would support the war effort with American technology and industrial might. Joseph Goebbels, the mastermind of German propaganda, wrote later that Hitler heard the speech, and so powerful were Churchill's words that Hitler saw images of farmers standing on the cliffs of Dover with axes and picks, ready to do battle against invading German ground forces. The speech convinced him that Germany should not attack Britain with infantry forces.[4] One speech galvanized Britain, convinced the American president and frightened the Nazi despot.

THE POWER OF WORDS

Looking at World War II as a war of words certainly validates Aristotle's claim of the power of speech: "The use of rational speech is more distinctive of a human being than the use of his limbs. . . . A man can confer the greatest of benefits by a right use of these, and inflict the greatest of injuries by using them wrongly."[5] Great benefit or great injury results from effective speech. That's why the Bible warns against the misuse of this gift:

> We all stumble in many ways. If anyone is never at fault in what he says, he is a perfect man, able to keep his whole body in check.
>
> When we put bits into the mouths of horses to make them obey us, we can turn the whole animal. Or take ships as an example. Although they are so large and are driven by strong winds, they are steered by a very small rudder wherever the pilot wants to go. Likewise the tongue is a small part of the body, but it makes great boasts. Consider what a great forest is set on fire by a small spark. The tongue also is a fire, a world of evil among the parts of the body. It corrupts the whole person, sets the whole course of his life on fire, and is itself set on fire by hell.
>
> All kinds of animals, birds, reptiles and creatures of the sea are being tamed and have been tamed by man, but no man can tame the tongue. It is a restless evil, full of deadly poison.
>
> With the tongue we praise our Lord and Father, and with it we curse men, who have been made in God's likeness. Out of the same mouth come praise and cursing. (Jas 3:2-10)

Consider the image James uses for the tongue. The tongue is a fire that can set a forest ablaze. It is uncontrollable and "a restless evil, full of deadly poison." It is also able to bless. The tongue, or human speech, makes poetry out of life, gives language to music and gives dialogue to love. What a gift when utilized for good!

GOOD WORDS

Civilizations found their meaning through the speech of leaders. In the earliest days of America, the revolutionary spirit was exemplified by Patrick Henry's famous words, "Is life so dear, or peace so sweet, as to be purchased at the price of chains and slavery? Forbid it, Almighty God! I know not what course others may take; but as for me, give me liberty or give me death!"

In the late twentieth century the words of John F. Kennedy ("Ask not what your country can do for you—ask what you can do for your country.") and Martin Luther King Jr. ("I have a dream that my four little children will one day live in a nation where they will not be judged by the color of their skin, but by the content of their character.") shaped the vision of a generation of Americans.

Nelson Mandela's words at his inaugural speech in 1994 calmed the anger of a repressed people and provided the framework for a peaceful revolution with dignity for all.

> We have triumphed in the effort to implant hope in the breasts of the millions of our people. We enter into a covenant that we shall build the society in which all South Africans, both black and white, will be able to walk tall, without any fear in their hearts, assured of their inalienable right to human dignity—a rainbow nation at peace with itself and the world.

Sometimes great speech is required to attack injustice and evil. When that speech comes from the lips of a person known for a life of love and dignity, the words cut even deeper into the souls of listeners. Consider the words of Mother Teresa before American leaders in 1994, many of whom disagreed strongly with her statement: "But I feel the greatest destroyer of peace today is abortion. . . . If we accept that a mother can kill even her own child, how can we tell other people not to kill one another? . . . We are fighting abortion by adoption—by care of the mother and adoption for her baby. . . . Please don't kill the child. I want the child. Please give me the child."[6]

Eyewitnesses still speak of the power of her words, given enormous credibility by her life, silencing the rhetoric of Washington, D.C.'s most powerful. President Clinton, who spoke after the diminutive nun, is reported to have said, "It is hard to argue against a life so well lived."

Speech has the power to influence thought by well-reasoned logic and emotionally passionate, authentic delivery. The values and visions of a society are shaped by ideas presented by the "preachers" of the day, who come from the many institutions of a society. Their ideas expressed through rhetoric carry great weight. Chuck Colson quotes philosopher Richard Weaver in his book *Ideas Have Consequences:* "It is the great ideas that inform the mind, fire the imagination, move the heart and shape a culture. History is little more than the recording of the rise and fall of the great ideas—the world views—that form our values and move us to act."[7]

GOD'S SPEECH

"God designed humans to be like himself, a communicator, one who reaches out, a builder of bridges. God designed people to talk!"[8]

God is not content to let the words of men and women shape the beliefs of people and societies. He gets into the act. In fact, it is the nature of God to speak. God spoke creation into being (see Gen 1:3, 6, 9, 11, 14, 20, 24, 26). God also spoke long ago by the prophets (see Heb 1:1). The record of the Old Testament shows God's empowerment of authorized speech through human beings. God's most important act was to speak to humankind through his Son, "whom he appointed heir of all things, and through whom he made the universe" (Heb 1:2). The message spoken by the Son was a message of salvation: "The time has come. . . . The kingdom of God is near. Repent and believe the good news"(Mk 1:15).

GOD SPEAKS THROUGH US

Perhaps most astonishing is the realization that God speaks through his followers today: "God was reconciling the world to himself in Christ, not counting men's sins against them. And he has committed to us the message of reconciliation. We are therefore Christ's ambassadors, as though God were making his appeal through us" (2 Cor 5:19-20). Therefore, through living heralds, God continues to speak. He speaks through us!

It is almost unbelievable that God would entrust his finest Word—Jesus—to us. Such is the mystery of God. And yet, knowing the power of speech, we shouldn't be surprised. God empowers our speech to reach deep into the souls of people. The great Boston pastor of the mid- to late-1800s, Phillips Brooks, said it best when he wrote that preaching is "truth through personality." But we need to take it one step further. Gospel preaching is God's truth poured through unique human beings who are filled with his own Spirit. There's nothing like it. We may not have the training of a classical actor. We may have less rhetorical power than a Kennedy or a King. But we have God speaking through us. In the end, that guarantees success.

This is a book about the God who speaks an imperative message through men and women who love and serve him. It is a book about God's special category of speech, which we call gospel proclamation. Through gospel proclamation, God thrusts the most important idea of civilization upon the world—namely, that forgiveness of sins and eternal life are offered to all people because of the life, death, resurrection and presence of Jesus Christ. Jesus was well aware that his life meant a new epoch had dawned on humankind: "The Spirit of the Lord is on me, because he has anointed me to preach good news to the poor. He has sent me to proclaim freedom for the prisoners and recovery of sight for the blind, to release the oppressed, to proclaim the year of the Lord's favor"(Lk 4:18-19).

REVIVING GOSPEL SPEECH (PROCLAMATION)

It is the view of the authors that gospel proclamation is in decline in much

of the Christian world, especially the West. Books on church growth, conferences on church leadership, and even missions gatherings and writings
give little ink or emphasis to gospel proclamation. This is a bit of a paradox,
really. While Billy Graham is revered throughout the world and larger
crowds than ever come to his events and the campaigns of others (such as
Luis Palau and Youth With A Mission's Impact World Tour), the general
talk seems to be that gospel preaching is archaic and ineffective. If it is valued at all, it is considered an addenda to other methods.

I (Lon) was in this latter camp early in my ministry career. Then God
taught me an interesting lesson in my first church plant. The congregation,
located in the Bay Area of northern California, was a great success by anyone's standards. Within four years, attendance was pushing toward nine
hundred. More important, scores (perhaps hundreds) were meeting Christ
each year. It truly was a church growing primarily because of conversion
rather than transfers and births.

At one point the staff decided to take a survey of attendees. We wanted
to know why people were coming to the church and what they most valued.
As a twenty-seven-year-old teaching pastor, I was quite sure I knew why the
people came: We were a church majoring on the arts. Each Sunday morning, a worship band with a distinct jazz flavor welcomed attendees. The
players in the band were topnotch. (One of our sax players played part time
for the Stan Kenton Orchestra. The bass player would someday win multiple Grammy awards.) And music was just the beginning. Multimedia slides
projected not only lyrics but also wonderful scenes of beauty (this was before PowerPoint and affordable video projection). Sometimes we sang songs
to stories depicted on the slides. The drama team brought a fresh sketch every week—a prelude to the message. Other Sundays found the dance team
interpreting a scriptural theme. And funniest of all was the puppet ministry.
Puppets can say things people only wish they could say. Yes, I knew why
people came. It was the full-blown artistic presentation of the gospel.

I was completely wrong. The number-one reason people attended was
to hear the twenty-five- to thirty-five-minute message. I couldn't believe it.

You see, I did most of the preaching. I knew how meager were my efforts and how poor was my handling of the Word of God. Years later I was told that Martin Luther always left the pulpit saying, "Phooey on you, Luther." That is how I felt every Sunday morning. Phooey on you, Lon. But I could not deny the results of our survey.

Dr. Jim Persson, my mentor who coplanted the church with me, put it all in perspective. After all, he was really old and wise, at least forty-five. He said, in essence, "I'm not surprised. God has always used gospel preaching to save people. He always will." That was a defining moment for me. I still say, "Phooey on you, Lon," but I do not deny the power of gospel proclamation. Since that time, the study of speech and especially of biblical gospel proclamation has been a centerpiece of my reflection and ministry practice.

We fully believe the gospel delivered through a Spirit-filled and trained vessel is riveting to listeners. We dare not underestimate the value of hearing someone make sense out of life, out of self and out of God in a twenty- to forty-minute miracle called preaching. Gospel preaching is an art form of incredible effect. We need restored confidence in gospel speech, a renewed commitment to excellence and then, most of all, the courage to *go public*.

PART 1

THE WONDER OF
PUBLIC PROCLAMATION

2

THE POWER OF
PUBLIC PROCLAMATION

Jeff Fountain, European director of YWAM, had just handed Mark the latest copy of *Newsweek*, and on the cover were the words, "Is God Dead?" The subtitle read, "In Western Europe, it sure can look that way." This July 12, 1999, European edition of *Newsweek* confirmed what I had personally witnessed all across this region of the world. People have abandoned church, and in many cases, even God.

Karen Armstrong writes in the *Newsweek* article, "If they give the subject any thought, many Swedes, Brits, French, Germans or Danes would say that they are glad to be rid of a deity who had threatened his adherents with hellfire, who had loomed over their lives like a cosmic big brother and who appeared to have made a terrible job of governing the world." She continues, "Nietzsche was right to say that human beings had killed God."

When reading this disturbing news, I had to ask, "How could this happen in a part of the world with such a rich history in the Christian faith?" What's equally alarming is that trends often begin in Europe and spread to the United States and the rest of the world.

All across Western Europe, church attendance has plummeted. Examine these numbers from the article, which show the percentage of regular church attendance in Europe from 1991 to 1998:

- West Germany—14.7 to 7 percent
- East Germany—3.6 to 2 percent
- Norway—4.6 to 4.1 percent

In France, only 4 percent of Parisians attend church regularly. In Great Britain, 99 percent of Church of England members didn't attend church in 1999, and only 11 percent of the population attends a church of any kind. The trends are the same in Italy and Ireland, primarily Roman Catholic nations.

The United States doesn't seem far behind. The *Harvesting Churches Newsletter* of November 15, 2000, stated that during the last century the church-population ratio has been declining.

Churches for every 10,000 Americans

Year	Number of Churches
1900	27 churches
1950	17 churches
1996	11 churches

Churches in the United States

	Per Week	Per Day
Losses	72.11	10.27
Gains	24.03	3.42
Net Loss	48.08	6.85

According to George Barna, a respected American researcher, in 1992 the median adult attendance per church service was 102. By 1995 it dropped to 95 and in 1999 it fell to 90—an 11-percent drop in seven years. Interestingly Barna found that during this same time the number of Christians sharing their faith also declined. Clearly there is a connection between church attendance and proclaiming Christ.

The question is, why is the church declining all over the Western world? While there are several components to this answer, one stands out: When the church turns inward, it dies. When it ceases to "go public" by being involved in the public debate for truth, it loses ground. When the primary focus becomes church life instead of the Great Commission to go, decline begins. This is true for an individual church as well as the church as a whole.

Holland is an example. YWAM is conducting evangelistic campaigns in the Netherlands. Church leaders there tell me (Mark) that evangelist T. L. Osborn held a great campaign there in 1958. During that multiweek outreach, an estimated 300,000 people heard the gospel. All across the nation, the press covered the outpouring of God in The Hague.

Recently I was in The Hague. The pastors proudly told me about the move of God that the Osborn meeting brought, and how they wish it could happen again. After this massive evangelistic thrust by Osborn, church attendance was strong and the church was growing. Today the Holland church as a whole is weak, with attendance at its low point. Church leaders tell me that regular Sunday service attendance is somewhere between 6 percent and 9 percent.

What happened? The church turned inward in the Netherlands, as it did in all of Western Europe. Discussion and emphasis turned to internal church activities, with less emphasis on reaching the lost. Since 1958 there's been very little public evangelism. In some church circles in Holland they even reject the idea of an altar call.

The heart of Jesus is to leave the ninety-nine to find the one who is lost. The entire purpose in Christ coming to this earth can be summarized in the statement, "The Son of Man came to seek and to save what was lost" (Lk 19:10). The New Testament is a manual on how to go, not how to stay. It was written to, and by, those who were fighting the good fight, advancing the gospel in a lost world. It was not written to a self-absorbed institution.

According to Jesus, the responsibility to influence change in the nations belongs to us.

"You are the salt of the earth. But if the salt loses its saltiness, how can it be made salty again? It is no longer good for anything, except to be thrown out and trampled by men.

"You are the light of the world. A city on a hill cannot be hidden. Neither do people light a lamp and put it under a bowl. Instead they put it on its stand, and it gives light to everyone in the house. In the same way, let your light shine before men, that they may see your good deeds and praise your Father in heaven." (Mt 5:13-16)

Disobedience to this command is the reason Christianity is declining in the Western world. It seems as if everyone but Christians are speaking in public forums. Week after week, secular music concerts fill our city auditoriums, holding "campaigns" that lead millions astray. Our media is filled with voices of lust, greed and rebellion. Our public schools promote a secular worldview. They use godless training leaving our children focused on self-gratification and pleasure. They teach a worldview where God is either irrelevant or nonexistent. With all of this going on, the church often seems oblivious. It seems content to be insulated within its four walls.

WHAT WENT WRONG?

Recently I (Mark) tried to explain to a group of church leaders in Denmark *why* the church has lost ground. In Denmark, church attendance is almost nonexistent. Leaders from around the country joined sixty-plus Bible college students to hear me speak at a four-day conference on church growth. The topics included instruction on relevant evangelism and what it takes to change a nation.

I explained that the gospel was prominent in Denmark at one time and the nation had been governed by biblical principles. The church was the primary influence in government, education, science, the arts, entertainment and almost every sphere of life, but over time this changed. The churches slowly ceased being the influence in society and grew content with a separate culture of their own. The result? Today if someone from the church world speaks up at all, he or she is ridiculed. Almost everyone in the general public considers the church antiquated and no longer relevant to other spheres of society.

The modern church in the West has two main problems: its *message* and its *method*. The message of the true gospel has been lost and is rarely preached anymore. This is true all over the Western world. (See chapter six, "The Lost Gospel.") The methods we use to present the gospel today are the same used in the last century. Unfortunately they no longer work as well in our time of high-tech, rapid change. In many cases the church has pulled out of everyday life and has retreated into a religious shell. Several generations of young people have grown up without a real understanding of what the Bible teaches and without a biblical worldview.

In that same seminar I explained to the pastors and Bible school students that the church cannot counter this deluge of secular thought with services that meet once a week. This method would never get the job done. It can never counteract all the influence the world brings.

HOW CAN WE REVERSE THE TREND?

I encouraged these church leaders to get back into the public, to be salt and light, to go to the airwaves, the marketplace of life—to bring the gospel of truth where people can hear it. I suggested that they stop building sanctuaries as we know them and begin erecting facilities that can be used seven days a week, and that they begin influencing areas like sports, the arts and the media. I explained, "The only way we can take back the ground we've lost is to go public, where people live."

On the morning of the second day of the seminar, one of the church leaders was quite upset with me. He stood up and began to challenge me: "I don't believe you. What we are doing is working!" I said, "Well, that might be true, but let's do a test. Let's find out if your present church structures and services are really working." He nodded his head in agreement. I continued, "We have more than a hundred people in this room, and many of you preached in a church last Sunday. How many of you remember the name of the sermon that you preached?" Twelve lifted their hands. "Let's go further," I said. "How many of you remember the main points?" Only two people out of more than one hundred could remember the main points of their own message. I continued, "How many of you saw the movie *Titanic?*" Almost everyone raised his or her hand. "How many of you can remember the main plot in the movie?" Again almost everyone raised his or her hand. Finally I asked, "How many can remember the theme song from the movie?" As many began to sing it, I said, "I rest my case."

For the first time, many began to realize that where they were investing their time and effort really wasn't changing society. They realized that the world is discipling us, we are not discipling the world. The problem wasn't that their worship services were unimportant, but that all of the church's life was lived within its four walls. The church was not present in the streets, the public auditoriums, on television and in the marketplaces of life. When Jesus said, "You are the light of the world," he clearly expected us to shine for people to see. We don't ask them to come to us; we go where they are.

What determines what people believe? The influences they are exposed to and the voices they hear. We all have 168 hours a week to spend. We sleep and eat for about 68 hours. That leaves us with about 100 discretionary hours.

Let's look at the average life of a sixteen-year-old in America. He or she watches thirty-nine hours of television a week, spends about twelve hours on the Internet and watching movies and videos, and gets about thirty-three hours of secular education. This only leaves about sixteen hours. How can the church compete with eighty-four hours of secular input? In its present form, it can't. Church attendance averages 2.2 times a month. Each service lasts about one hour and twenty minutes. The average sermon is about thirty minutes long. And that's only if the person is involved in church life, and most young people are not. As someone with a marketing background, I can tell you that the day after hearing a sermon, the average person only remembers about 6 percent of it. We shouldn't be surprised to learn that the young people who attend church in the Western world have very little understanding of the Word of God.

CHANGED DOWN UNDER

In 1994 while we were in Australia preparing to launch our first citywide campaign in that nation, I met with Tom Hallis, YWAM's Asia-Pacific regional leader. Tom is an old Aussie who seems to know everyone in Australia. I asked him, "What do you think of our campaigns?" He answered, "I think this is great! It's about time. The Graham campaigns changed the nation." Now he had my attention. "What do you mean?" I asked.

He explained that Billy Graham had begun his campaigns in 1959, packing out stadiums all over the nation. People who couldn't attend listened on radio. Then Tom said something I've never forgotten: "Half the preachers in the pulpits today are a result of those campaigns." Later I found out that he was speaking about the cumulative effect of the 1959, 1968 and 1969 campaigns. In his personal research, Tom discovered that the call of many church leaders in Australia today traces back to decisions made at these events. Many other Australian church leaders confirmed his findings. In the 1959 campaign, Graham crisscrossed the nation: Melbourne, Sydney, Perth, Adelaide and Brisbane. Associate evangelists reached into the smaller cities, schools and prisons. In all, about 3.3 million people heard the gospel, with 150,000 decisions for Christ. It did indeed change the nation.

A STATE TRANSFORMED

I watched a similar phenomenon in my (Mark's) work in India. In 1984 the ministry I founded called Church on the Move conducted campaigns in Andhra Pradesh. A state of about sixty million people, Andhra is primarily Hindu, Muslim and animist.

I sent to Andhra my nephew, Scott Norling, and his young friend Eric Hanson, who were both on our staff. They spent three months acclimating to the culture and then began preparing for our first campaigns. From our first outreaches in 1984 through 1991, we held or facilitated about twenty urban campaigns and averaged about five village outreaches each week. From the campaigns came many church plants, a medical clinic, Christian schools, literacy programs and a host of other initiatives. Millions heard the gospel, with hundreds of thousands of decisions for Christ.

Our work in the 1980s, along with my nephew's continued public proc-

lamation through his own ministry with India Gospel Mission, impacted
Andhra Pradesh. The Christian population in the state has grown signifi-
cantly, especially in the areas where we worked the hardest with proclamation evangelism. Of course, we know God has many other workers in the
area, but according to Chandra Bose, our Indian director at that time, the
advances in Andhra in both church membership and number of churches
are in proportion to the public evangelism that we did.

Bose remains one of the most significant church leaders in the state. He
holds a doctorate in theology as well as a law degree. His wife, Leela, has
been a professor at a local Christian university for many years. Bose inter-
acts regularly with denominational leaders throughout the region. According to his research, in the districts where we conducted the largest number
of campaigns, the overall church population grew the most. This included
the districts of Krishna, Kurnool, Guntur, Nellore, Nalgonda, Warangal,
Karimnagar, Khammam, Godvari and Medak.

While research in this Third World nation is incredibly difficult, Bose
and his associates have estimated that the Christian population in these areas has almost tripled since 1984. Church plants directly related to the evangelistic campaigns number in the hundreds. Even with this dramatic
growth in the number of Christians, we need to increase the amount of
public evangelism with corresponding church planting. The population of
India is growing by twenty-eight million people per year, and most have still
not heard the gospel.

AND THIS GOSPEL MUST BE PROCLAIMED

The apostle Paul asks a series of questions: "How can they believe in the
one of whom they have not heard? And how can they hear without someone preaching to them? And how can they preach unless they are sent?"
(Rom 10:14-15). People cannot change unless they hear truth, and they
can't hear truth unless someone goes to them. This charge to Christians
is not about getting people to come to us. It is about bringing the message to them. Throughout history, God has used public proclamation to

shape society. We can win our communities if we'll return to using this powerful tool.

Recently, evangelist Luis Palau related to an audience of emerging evangelists that when he was ten his family passed out gospel literature from the back of an old pickup truck in Buenos Aires. Evangelicals, he reminisced, were few in those days. The tracts were a faithful witness to a very few. He added that in the spring of 2003, at the age of sixty-eight, he proclaimed Christ to more than one million people in the same city. With centers of commerce and government in the background, Palau proclaimed faithfully to the masses. He met privately with government and business leaders. Many thousands came to Christ. What a contrast to those early days of "pickup" evangelism!

God is faithful to his Word—it will not return void. Public proclamation is a great megaphone for the truth. May our confident, passionate and loving voices declare Christ in the public forums of our world.

3

BIBLICAL FOUNDATIONS OF PUBLIC PROCLAMATION

It happened during a time of Bible study and prayer. I (Mark) was reading Acts 2, a portion of Scripture I had read many times before. But this time it was different. The story of the birth of the church on Pentecost came alive. I saw things I had never noticed before. For example, the first church was born out of an evangelistic campaign. I had been taught that churches plant other churches, usually using small groups of some kind to initiate them. This is common, of course, but Acts 2 gave a different model.

Another thing that struck me was the fact that God used an evangelist, Peter, to birth the first Christian church. The models I had studied on church planting up to this point used pastors as the church planters, not evangelists.

The original converts to Christianity were not the result of one-on-one ministry or small group meetings; rather they were reached by large-scale public evangelism. God chose this impersonal form of witness to start his church.

On that day of Pentecost, Peter called the crowd to repentance, pleading with them, "Save yourselves from this corrupt generation" (Acts 2:40). And "those who accepted his message were baptized, and about three thousand were added to their number that day" (v. 41).

It's interesting that God chose Peter, the disciple whose character most epitomizes the office of the evangelist, at least the ones I have known—bold, sometimes loud and uninhibited, and the quickest to say yes to Jesus.

Often they are impulsive, much like a bull in a china shop, and not very polished. They can be easily misunderstood and frequently are controversial. Public evangelists are sometimes revered, like Billy Graham in his later years, but usually are misunderstood, like Billy in his younger days.

A case in point was my own experience while being grafted into Youth With A Mission, a very large discipleship-oriented ministry. I didn't start out as many YWAMers do, as an inexperienced nineteen-year-old in a Discipleship Training School. I became a YWAMer after fifteen years of missions and ministry, having already traveled much of the world.

In 1994 Loren Cunningham, cofounder of YWAM, asked me to speak to the global leadership of the mission during the Delhi consultation. He did this to introduce me to the more than two hundred key veterans in this organization. Little did I know how controversial I would be.

I was one of many speaking in workshops at this two-week conference. My session wasn't until Tuesday of the second week. I used the first few days to get to know my new missions family. People were gracious and went out of their way to introduce themselves to me. After exchanging names, they usually asked me what I did. Of course I answered, "I conduct citywide evangelistic campaigns in cities around the world." The most common response I got was, "Oh, really?"—often followed by a sudden change of subject. By the end of the first day of the conference, I came to realize I didn't fit their definition of a missionary. There were, of course, exceptions, but these were rare.

On the second day, Dean Sherman, a respected veteran in YWAM, asked to have lunch with me. While we were eating, Dean said, "So you do mass evangelism? There aren't many evangelists in YWAM." After a pause, he asked, "Do you know why?" Not waiting for a response, he answered his own question: "Because we're a discipling organization." I really didn't know what to say. I couldn't tell if he was for me or against me. His next words set me at ease: "We need people like you. Evangelism has to move back into the forefront of YWAM as it was in our early days."

Over the next hour, Dean and I had a spirited conversation about my call into YWAM. It left me with two distinct messages. One, I was an aberration in this discipling organization; YWAM had many different ministries, but was largely a short-term missions and training organization. Two, God had called me here.

Because I would only have one hour to introduce myself and make my case for the role of public proclamation, I prayed about what I would say in my session. The Lord gave me an idea.

I walked back into the hotel, found the maintenance room and asked to borrow a toolbox. Then I went back outside and found a large rock. Half an hour later I was introduced as an evangelist new to YWAM. After greeting the audience, I called two of the biggest men to the front to help me. I handed them each two small screwdrivers from the toolbox and asked them to break the rock on the table. They began pounding away on the rock with the screwdrivers. After a minute or so, it was clear they were making no headway. All they were doing was hurting their hands. I thanked them and let them return to their seats.

Then I said, "There are different tools for different jobs. If you're going to fix a television, you need fine instruments like these small screwdrivers. But if you're going to break a rock, you need something different." I then reached back into the toolbox and pulled out a fifteen-pound hammer. I lifted it above my head and slammed it down on the rock, shattering the rock into dozens of pieces. Then I read Jeremiah 23:29: "'Is not my word like fire,' declares the LORD, 'and like a hammer that breaks a rock in pieces?'"

I continued, "I do the work of an evangelist, the hammer in God's toolbox. I proclaim the Word of God publicly, boldly and with spiritual force. God's Word applied in this fashion can shatter strongholds. You may not use a hammer to fix a television, but it's more effective when you're breaking rocks." I spent the rest of the hour explaining how I have used public proclamation and closed my session by giving all two hundred participants a miniature hammer to use as a paperweight to remind them of the need to include this gift in their missions plans.

Operating as a bold, uncompromising evangelist, Peter shook up Jerusalem with his preaching. He was the hammer God used that day to birth the church. His direct message on sin and forgiveness moved the listeners to deep repentance, thus creating a strong foundation for their new life in Christ.

LIFE-CHANGING CONVERSIONS

Those who gave themselves to Christ on Pentecost "devoted themselves to the apostles' teaching and to the fellowship, to the breaking of bread and to prayer" (Acts 2:42). The quality of these new converts was remarkable. But many who claim to be authorities on church growth and discipleship will tell you that only personal and small group evangelism work. They further teach that there are no lasting results when large numbers respond to Christ in a big campaign. In some of these teaching circles, the words *mass evangelism* are like curse words, certainly not part of the vocabulary of someone serious about making disciples. (We speak more of this in chapter eight, "Seeking Relevance.")

According to Acts 2:43-47, these three thousand new converts to Christianity, all saved in a single day through public proclamation, were seemingly ideal Christians.

- "Everyone was filled with awe, and many wonders and miraculous signs were done by the apostles." (It was a supernatural church.)

- "All the believers were together and had everything in common." (It was a generous church.)

- "They broke bread in their homes and ate together with glad and sincere hearts, praising God." (It was a grateful church.)

- "And the Lord added to their number daily those who were being saved." (It was a growing church.)

God was giving me the biblical pattern I had prayed for. What I was reading excited but also deeply bothered me. The exciting part was knowing it would work today just as it had in Bible times. What bothered me was the fact that much of the church in the Western world had moved away from public proclamation as an instrument in changing nations, thus departing from this key biblical pattern.

In the weeks that followed, I spent many hours studying the book of Acts. What emerged from my study was what I call the Acts Model—a recurring pattern used by the apostles to expand the early church throughout the region of Asia Minor in their lifetimes. I knew God wanted me to pattern my new evangelistic ministry after what he had shown me in the book of Acts.

For years, the Billy Graham Evangelistic Association has organized its evangelistic campaigns using three phases: *preparation, proclamation* and *preservation*. They estimate that in their campaigns, 45 percent of the efforts are in preparation, 45 percent in preservation and 10 percent in the event, or the proclamation phase. This is similar to the pattern the Lord opened up to me as I studied the ministry of Jesus and the early apostles. The following paragraphs describe those three phases.

Phase 1: Preparation. Jesus worked three and a half years preparing his disciples for the day of his departure. He knew they would have to manage the church and care for the new converts. This preparation had two parts: organizational and spiritual. Complete preparation will always contain these two elements. His teaching included how to operate in his kingdom by conducting strategic warfare and prayer (spiritual). He also taught how to manage and care for large crowds (organizational).

One example of organizational training is the instructions Jesus gave his disciples during the feeding of the five thousand in Bethsaida. This large crowd had followed Jesus into a remote area without giving thought to food or lodging. The disciples pointed out this problem to the Master, and Jesus used this need as an opportunity to teach them how to manage and care for large crowds. He replied, "You give them something to eat." The disciples let him know that they had only five loaves of bread and two fish and that they could not afford to feed all those people (about five thousand men, not to mention women and children). Jesus directed them to have the people sit down in groups. The disciples did so. He then blessed the loaves and fish, giving them back to the disciples to distribute to the people. To their great surprise, it fed everyone, with twelve baskets left over.

This kind of organizational training no doubt proved valuable later in overseeing the many thousands who came to Christ through their public witness. Before ascending into heaven, Jesus told five hundred disciples to "wait for the gift my Father promised," the baptism of the Holy Spirit (Acts 1:4). He also promised, "You will receive power when the Holy Spirit comes on you; and you will be my witnesses" (v. 8), teaching them the importance of faith and seeking God. We find the disciples in the Upper Room praying constantly, waiting for what Jesus promised. Their hunger was rewarded just days later at Pentecost.

Phase 2: Proclamation (public proclamation and demonstration of truth). We cannot have the same results as the early church without going public in our preaching. The world will not be reached only by witnessing one-on-one to the lost. While this should be the lifestyle of every true believer, it cannot replace proclamation in the public domain. Jesus made this clear by what he did and what he taught. His ministry included public preaching on an almost daily basis, usually in front of large crowds in the synagogue courts or in the marketplaces. The same is true of his disciples; the book of Acts is literally filled with story after story describing the apostles preaching in public.

Notice these words of Jesus: "You are the light of the world. A city on a hill cannot be hidden. Neither do people light a lamp and put it under a bowl. Instead they put it on its stand, and it gives light to everyone in the house" (Mt 5:14-15). The phrase "a city on a hill" depicts shining our light from a public place for all to see. I have always questioned the idea of a "personal" or "private" faith. Faith in Christ should be very public. Jesus went so far as to say, "Whoever acknowledges me before men, I will also acknowledge him before my Father in heaven. But whoever disowns me before men, I will disown him before my Father" (Mt 10:32-33). Biblical faith is public faith.

A comprehensive study of the book of Acts shows the apostles moving from city to city, proclaiming Christ in the most public of places. It seemed wherever they could find the largest crowd, that's where they would preach. This often created stirs and confrontations, but that's the effect truth has on people. Because truth by nature is absolute, it either persuades or condemns the listener. The writer of Hebrews tells us, "For the word of God is living and active. Sharper than any double-edged sword, it penetrates even to dividing soul and spirit, joints and marrow, it judges the thoughts and attitudes of the heart. Nothing in all creation is hidden from God's sight. Everything is uncovered and laid bare before the eyes of him to whom we must give account" (4:12-13). I believe many Christians back off from public proclamation of truth so they will avoid confrontations. Too many of us in the Western world seem to be content to keep the truth within the four walls of our church buildings, avoiding the confrontation that often accompanies proclamation in public.

We see by Peter's example on the day of Pentecost that *effective* evangelistic preaching needs several elements. First, it should be accompanied by the supernatural demonstration of God's presence. (We speak of this more in chapter nine, "The Demonstration of Truth.") Second, we must use crosscultural communication. In Acts 2, those assembled from all over Asia were able to hear the message in their own tongue. This required miraculous intervention, but the principle applies to any audience. If the listener doesn't understand the language we are using, then we are not really communicating. Third, Peter was bold and direct. He confronted sin, called for repentance and challenged his audience to completely surrender to Jesus. We cover this also in chapter six.

Phase 3: Preservation (discipling). We notice a continuation of signs and wonders: "Everyone was filled with awe, and many wonders and miraculous signs were done by the apostles" (Acts 2:43). New Christians need this supernatural environment. Often someone is converted in a large gathering where the presence of God is strong, but afterward is asked to attend a Bible study or church service with little or no sense of God's presence or power.

Older churchgoers may be able to accept programs that lack God's supernatural presence, but new Christians usually are not. They were converted by the power of God and want to continue to live by that same power. They want to follow a God who is awesome and amazing. The tangible presence of the Lord and extraordinary love for the world marked the first New Testament church. Christ's church should have the same characteristics today.

While evangelism can be done very effectively in a large-group setting, long-term discipling is better done on a more personal level. In Acts 2:46, notice the setting of their gatherings: "Every day they continued to meet together in the temple courts. They broke bread in their homes and ate together with glad and sincere hearts." These were culturally appropriate settings for discipling someone in Peter's day. Notice that they also broke bread together—another cultural component. The more of these culturally relevant elements we can include in follow-up, the more effective we will be. My marketing background taught me that the common elements of culture are age, gender, language, values, ethnicity and customs.

If we take time to study the culture of the people to whom we are ministering, we can provide relevant environments for discipleship. The typical church culture is not attractive to most new converts, particularly young people and children. According to a World Vision study, 87 percent of those who come to Christ are under eighteen years of age. Most churches are filled with forty- to seventy-year-olds; thus the programs naturally cater to these ages and often miss the culture of the youth. This is a primary reason it is difficult to get young people into church life.

True discipleship is not a program but rather a daily relationship with someone we care about. It's not handing someone an advertisement to come to church or sending a mailing; it's not a stranger calling to invite people to attend something. It's breaking bread at a common table. Getting new converts immediately *into* the church is less important than getting the body of Christ *out* of the church to disciple people where they live.

The Acts Model with all three of these elements—preparation, proclamation, preservation—provides an effective framework to achieve our stated goals: to reach and disciple the lost.

PAUL'S INSTRUCTIONS

As seen above, the preaching of the gospel was modeled by Christ and practiced as a chief vehicle for evangelism throughout the early church period. That the first disciples would give preaching such a place of prominence should not surprise us. They had watched the Lord Jesus preach the good news for nearly three years. But perhaps more importantly, they remembered his final admonition to them. Using the Old Testament Scriptures as his basis, Jesus said, "This is what is written: The Christ will suffer and rise from the dead on the third day, and repentance and forgiveness of sins will be preached in his name to all nations, beginning at Jerusalem" (Lk 24:46-47).

This is the command that all followers of Christ carry in their spiritual DNA. We are called to proclaim, or preach, this message to all ethnicities throughout the world. How good it is to know that the gospel preached transcends all cultures. Evidently both the message about Christ and the means of communicating the message—preaching—will work in every place at every time.

The word *proclaim* is usually translated "preach" and is the clearest word in the Greek language for formal speech. It literally means to "announce, make known by a herald, to proclaim aloud."[1] The word was used in the Greek world for public address and became the dominant word for "preach" in the New Testament.

Public proclamation is not only practiced and modeled by Christ and the first apostles, it is also taught or prescribed as important in the Epistles. In his letters, Paul expounded on the command of Christ, giving theological rationale for gospel speech. These are timeless truths that live throughout the centuries and are as valid today as in the first century.

Paul makes the point that salvation is available to all people:

> But what does it say? "The word is near you; it is in your mouth and in your heart," that is, the word of faith we are proclaiming: That if you confess with your mouth, "Jesus is Lord," and believe in your

heart that God raised him from the dead, you will be saved. For it is with your heart that you believe and are justified, and it is with your mouth that you confess and are saved. As the Scripture says, "Anyone who trusts in him will never be put to shame." For there is no difference between Jew and Gentile—the same Lord is Lord of all and richly blesses all who call on him, for, "Everyone who calls on the name of the Lord will be saved."

How, then, can they call on the one they have not believed in? And how can they believe in the one of whom they have not heard? And how can they hear without someone preaching to them? And how can they preach unless they are sent? As it is written, "How beautiful are the feet of those who bring good news!"

But not all the Israelites accepted the good news. For Isaiah says, "Lord, who has believed our message?" Consequently, faith comes from hearing the message, and the message is heard through the word of Christ. (Rom 10:8-17)

The conditions for salvation are believing that Christ is raised, and thereby present and active in the Word, and placing oneself in service to Christ as Lord (v. 9; Christ has absolute authority in one's life). The means for receiving the knowledge of this salvation is through gospel speech, or public proclamation. Paul uses the same Greek word for *proclaim* as Luke. Using a rhetorical pattern, Paul argues that, in fact, belief cannot occur unless there is gospel speech (see v. 14). Proclamation is the conduit for salvation. Through proclamation, the gospel is clarified for listeners. In theology, we speak of this clarifying nature as "specific" revelation. God witnesses of himself through creation (see Rom 1:18-20) and also through the demonstration of truth, namely acts of love and signs and wonders. But these comprise general revelation. It takes proclamation to clarify the gospel.

In light of this, it shouldn't surprise us that Paul viewed proclamation as the highest priority in his own ministry. In 1 Corinthians 1:17-21 he wrote,

For Christ did not send me to baptize, but to preach the gospel—not with words of human wisdom, lest the cross of Christ be emptied of its power.

For the message of the cross is foolishness to those who are perishing, but to us who are being saved it is the power of God. For it is written: "I will destroy the wisdom of the wise; the intelligence of the intelligent I will frustrate."

Where is the wise man? Where is the scholar? Where is the philosopher of this age? Has not God made foolish the wisdom of the world? For since in the wisdom of God the world through its wisdom did not know him, God was pleased through the foolishness of what was preached to save those who believe.

Factions and dissension were occurring in Corinth. Evidently the person who conducted a believer's baptism became the leader of the believer's life. Therefore some followed Peter, others Apollos. Paul thought that was nonsense. To him the role of baptizer meant nothing. What mattered was Christ, and him proclaimed. Paul understood that many would doubt the power and effect of gospel speech. In the same chapter, he admitted that some would consider the gospel best contained in written form ("Where is the scribe?" v. 20, NASB). Others thought the good news was best communicated in formal teaching settings ("Where is the debater?" v. 20, NASB). Still others thought God could best make his point through amazing signs and wonders (v. 22). But God chose gospel speech. It seemed almost foolish, but proclamation was God's chosen means (v. 21). In his paraphrase of the Bible, *The Message*, Eugene Peterson translates verse 21 well: "God in his wisdom took delight in using what the world considered dumb—*preaching*, of all things!—to bring those who trust him into the way of salvation."

It is a bit comforting to know that even in Paul's day people thought preaching was a "dumb" way for God to make a point. We don't know any Christian leaders that consider public proclamation dumb as much as they consider it passé. You hear things like, "It had its day, but this is the era of [fill in the blank with the latest trend] evangelism," or "The Billy Graham and T. L. Osborne eras are past," or "Postmoderns won't listen to preaching; it's too authoritarian and impersonal," or "In the world of technology, people won't go to public settings to be preached at." We've heard all these and other complaints, but argue that relevant public gospel speech is as effective today as in any era of the church.

More importantly, our view is that effective and relevant public proclamation, or gospel speech, is modeled and mandated by Christ himself, practiced by the apostles and prescribed by Paul repeatedly. It was the dominant means of gospel delivery in the New Testament. The ways we preach the gospel may change, but its power is undiminished by time. The three phases of preparation, proclamation and preservation provide a clear pattern to follow; these principles work in any place and time.

In the next chapter we fly through church history looking for notable examples of public gospel proclamation. It is a whirlwind of a journey, but we believe it's worth the ride.

4

THE HISTORY OF PUBLIC PROCLAMATION

This sentence reads like a majestic formal oration: "In the past God spoke to our forefathers through the prophets at many times and in various ways, but in these last days he has spoken to us by his Son, whom he appointed heir of all things, and through whom he made the universe" (Heb 1:1-2). The author wanted his first words about the Lord Jesus Christ to ring with glory, and they do. God has always spoken to us—first in the act of creation, then through his prophets in the epoch of the Old Testament. Now he speaks to us through his Son. We are in the age between the first and second advent of Christ, and this text suggests the Son is still speaking. It is in "these" last days he speaks. He who created all things is still in the act of creating, but now he creates life through the new birth in human hearts. Note that speech is the vehicle of his communication. And how does the Son speak? In many ways, not the least of which is through his people. Hear the pronouncement of Paul: "We are therefore Christ's ambassadors, as though God were making his appeal through us" (2 Cor 5:20). And Peter: "If anyone speaks, he should do it as one speaking the very words of God" (1 Pet 4:11).

In a marvelous sense, the Christian speaker/evangelist carries on this grand tradition of speaking for God. Throughout the ages, the Son has spoken through his servants the message that carries the good news of a new creation. What a privilege! Contemporary artist Ron DiCianni created a wonderful picture titled "The Legacy" of a preacher standing in his pulpit, holding the Scriptures and speaking to his audience. On both sides of him, invisible to the preacher and audience, but evident to viewers of the painting, are two lines of prophets, apostles and unknown others who proclaimed before him. They are the cloud of preachers in whose shadow we stand.

In this chapter we attempt the impossible. In one grand sweep we will seek to outline the tradition of gospel speech through the centuries.[1] It is a fine and noble tradition. While we limit our view of church history by looking at it only through the lens of evangelistic preaching, we are not saying preaching was solely responsible for the maintenance and growth of the Christian faith. Through the ages, God has used many means to fuel the church. For instance, many revivals and awakenings had strong movements of prayer at their center. The Reformation utilized a return to biblical theology for its vitality. Some eras witnessed a Spirit-led commitment to social action. But with all these God-ordained activities, strong gospel preaching had a place. Sometimes it defined an era; other times it was just a part of God's activity.

If you have not read much church history, some of the names and times may be confusing. Don't be concerned. Simply let God's faithfulness through history give you all the more confidence that he can use you today as his mouthpiece. In fact, you'll see more attention given to the era we call the First Great Awakening (early 1700s) because the authors have been so inspired by stories from that time. We admit a limitation in that most of our information comes from Western civilization. For that we apologize and encourage others to tell stories from their own tradition and cultures.

APOSTOLIC ERA

Gospel speech through the church begins with the apostles and the early believers. It is valuable to look at Peter and Paul for the motivation for—and trust in—proclamation as the primary vehicle for the gospel. Listen to Peter's boldness and confidence in his first address in Acts 2 as he begins, "Fellow Jews and all of you who live in Jerusalem, let me explain this to you; listen carefully to what I say" (v. 14). Peter believed the spoken word contained vital information for the lives of a whole city. His passion urges his audience to listen to the words. Oh, that we as preachers held, as did Peter, that the message—both in its content and its delivery—really matters to the world. Nothing has changed today, except our general lack of confidence in the message and the role of the messenger. Peter would have been appalled at such.

Paul held similar views. He was built to preach, at least in his own mind. He links his calling to the task of gospel speech: "God, who set me apart from birth and called me by his grace, was pleased to reveal his Son in me *so that I might preach him among the Gentiles*" (Gal 1:15-16, emphasis added). Though tempted to throw his considerable energies into other fields, including tent making, baptizing and administrating a global mission, Paul held strongly that his first task was to proclaim Christ, "for Christ did not send me to baptize, but to preach the gospel" (1 Cor 1:17). We see this call lived out in his eagerness to proclaim and utilize his gift: "I long to see you so that I may impart to you some spiritual gift to make you strong. . . . *That is why I am so eager to preach the gospel also to you* who are at Rome. I am not ashamed of the gospel, because it is the power of God" (Rom 1:11, 15-16, emphasis added).

Peter and Paul, as well as Stephen, Philip and other New Testament leaders, saw gospel speech as primary to fulfilling the command of Jesus to go to all the world and make disciples. As Haddon Robinson says, "To the NT writers, preaching stands as the event through which God works."[2] Perhaps this attitude is best summed up by the brief aside in Acts 5: "Day after day, in the temple courts and from house to house, they never stopped teaching and proclaiming the good news that Jesus is the Christ" (v. 42). We hope this focus can be reawakened—day by day and without ceasing.

A.D. 100-450

With the example of first-century believers to guide them, it is no wonder the church fathers carried the tradition forward with great energy. The growth of the church was phenomenal. Sociologist Rodney Stark believes there were only about 7,500 believers by the year 100. But between

100 and 350, the time of Constantine, the church grew 40 percent per decade, resulting in more than thirty-three million Christians. This represented more than half of the Roman Empire.[3] Stark writes that by the time Constantine decreed the empire would be Christian, it was already a foregone conclusion. He was merely stating a fact, not declaring a religious direction.

Great gospel preaching was an important aspect of this era of overwhelming growth. In his classic history of the Roman Empire, Edward Gibbon observed that "the custom of preaching, which seems to constitute a considerable part of Christian devotion was to be found everywhere in the Roman Empire." He also wrote, "The pulpits of the empire were now filled with sacred orators who possessed the advantage of not being questioned without danger of interruption or reply."[4]

To mention a few of the luminaries of this era, we start with Irenaeus (circa 135-202). As Bishop of Lyon in the Rhone Valley, his preaching put great weight on the doctrine of Christ and Christus Victor. He preached in outdoor markets as well as villages, and God used his ministry to establish the church in southern France.[5] Origen (circa 185-254) preached every day. He is often remembered as the father of allegory and had some heretical ideas, such as the denial of the bodily resurrection of Christ. However, he held strongly that Christ was the means of salvation. And he argued in favor of itinerant preaching. Concerning the value he placed on preaching, he wrote:

All in whom Christ speaks, that is to say every upright man and preacher who speaks the word of God to bring men to salvation—and not merely the apostles and prophets—can be called an arrow of God. But what is sad, I see very few arrows of God. There are so few who so speak as to inflame the heart of the hearer, drag him away from his sin, and convert him to repentance. Few so speak that the heart of their hearers is deeply convicted and his eyes weep for contrition. There are so few who unveil the light of the future hope, the wonder and glory of God's Kingdom to such effect that by their earnest preaching they succeed in persuading men to despise the visible and seek the invisible, to spurn the temporal and seek the eternal. There are all too few preachers of this caliber.[6]

How we long to see more "arrows of God." Don't Origen's words have as much conviction today as they did more than seventeen hundred years ago? We believe God desires to raise up an army of "preachers of this caliber."

One cannot leave the first five centuries of the church without mentioning at least the names of Chrysostom (also known as John of Antioch, 343-407) and Augustine (354-470). Chrysostom, a nickname meaning "golden-mouthed," was a spellbinding preacher and one-time archbishop of Constantinople. Though he and Augustine were perhaps less evangelistic than the fathers before them (they lived in a largely Christian empire), their preaching nonetheless presented Christ through the Scriptures with great power and regularity. Augustine was a professor of rhetoric before becoming a believer and was a master of speech. Like Origen, he preached without manuscript or notes. During his life he wrote 230 books. Most historians consider him the first source after the Scriptures for the church for the next thousand years. Yet with all his powers of thought and speech, Augustine once wrote:

> My preaching almost always displeases me. For I am eager after something better, of which I often have an inward enjoyment before I set about expressing my thought in audible words. Then, when I have failed to utter my meaning as clearly as I conceived it, I am disappointed that my tongue is incapable of doing justice to that which is in my heart.[7]

Don't all of us who hold in our minds the Word of God and the mystery of Christ cry out to God with the same passion? And yet God continues to use his preached Word for the miraculous act of salvation. How good to know that those who went before us, long before us, labored under the same anxieties.

A.D. 450-1500

The Roman Empire was collapsing and ushering the world into what is pessimistically called the Dark Ages. The Dark, or Middle, Ages comprise a thousand years of history from approximately 450 to 1450. As Rome declined, the Byzantine Empire rose, and following quickly, so did Islamic civilization. Christianity in this era is known less for what it was for, than what it was against. Manichaeism, Pelagianism and other heretical views caught many ears. In some ways, arguing for the Christian faith, and even fighting for it (the Crusades), replaced proclamation and its goal to persuade. The church focused more on purifying the church than on reaching the lost of the world. Use of the Scriptures declined.

A notable light in this era was the rise of monastic movements. While we often wrongly accuse monastics of ignoring the world, they did much to keep the spirituality of Christianity vibrant. As arts and letters declined in culture, the church took over education. Sadly this education was limited to the privileged male, and soon only the upper classes and the clergy were educated. Another notable but sad reality of this era was the Crusades, as northern Europeans carrying the banner of the cross sought to liberate the Holy Land from Islamic control. Both sides perpetrated evil and sorrows. This is the saddest era of the church. Yet, however dark the age, however dim the light, there still was some light. Out of the West came the Celtic believers to reevangelize the dying Roman world.

St. Patrick is best known of the preacher-missionaries of the early-fifth century. Born in Britain, he was captured by Celtic pirates at age sixteen and served as a slave for six years. In those years of Irish captivity, Patrick shepherded flocks and, like David, found fellowship with the God of creation. Dr. George Hunter suggests that, while in exile, the young Patrick learned the language and culture of the Celtic tribes, especially their love of creation and artistic expression. More than all, he came to love the people.[8] After his escape and return to Britain, he was ordained into the priesthood and served his land of birth until age forty-eight. At an age exceeding life expectancy for that era, Patrick received a call to bring the gospel to Ireland. He was ordained as bishop and returned with a team of assistants to the land of his slavery.

Patrick's pattern was to bring small teams into villages and live among the people, building relationships of trust. Then the gospel was proclaimed in regular settings, followed by the establishment of a local church. By the end of his life, Patrick had witnessed thousands of baptisms, perhaps tens of thousands. Seven hundred village churches were planted, one thousand priests ordained, and it is surmised that nearly 25 percent of Ireland's 150 tribes were thoroughly Christianized. Social reform was also a topic of Patrick. As far as we know, he was the first public preacher to speak out against slavery.[9]

The "fire from Ireland," as David Larsen aptly describes it, did not conclude with Patrick.[10] Columba, St. Ninian, Aidan and others carried the gospel and civilization to Scandinavia and then to all of western Europe. Unusual for the Middle Ages, Celtic Christians evangelized with great fervor, combining a passion for Christ with learning that was impossible to deny.

Gregory the Great (540-604) was made Bishop of Rome in 590. He sought to reform the priesthood and restore the high value of preaching.

> For it is true that whosoever enters on the priesthood undertakes the office of herald, so as to walk, himself crying aloud, before the coming of the judge who follows terribly. Wherefore, if the priest knows not how to preach, what voice of a loud cry shall the mute herald utter? For hence it is that the Holy Spirit sat upon the first pastors under the appearances of tongues (Acts 2:3); because whomsoever He has filled, He himself at once makes eloquent.[11]

Gregory was a great preacher himself, a master storyteller and one who felt the imminent return of the Lord Jesus. "Be watchful and alert!" he wrote. "Those who love God should shout for joy at the end of the world. . . . The world grows old and hoary, and through a sea of troubles hastens to approaching death."[12]

One of the finest examples of monastic preachers is St. Bernard of Clairvaux (1091-1153). Luther later wrote of him as the "most pious of all the monks." He penned that Bernard "preached Christ most charmingly. I follow him wherever he preached Christ, and I pray to Christ in the faith in which he prayed to Christ."[3] Bernard's preaching also evidenced itself in another communicative art form: music. We remember him for the great hymns "O Sacred Head Now Wounded" and "Jesus, the Very Thought of Thee."

Francis of Assisi (1182-1226) brought a further dimension to preaching by insisting that preachers live the life they preach. Once he converted the bandits that robbed him. Larsen says, "He stressed the prayers and tears of those who would win others to Christ." His advice to proclaimers is as valuable today as a thousand years ago: "I warn and remind friars that whenever they preach, their words are to be well chosen and pure, so as to help and edify the people, and to define virtues and vices, punishment and glory. And let them be brief, for the Lord Himself while on earth was brief."[4] Many of our audiences would advise us to pay heed to Francis regarding brevity. I (Lon) recall a gifted preacher giving me the same counsel his pilot brother had given him: "If after ten minutes you're still on the runway and not in the air, shut her down."

The church clearly held culture in the West together during the Middle Ages. As those years concluded, sorrows filled the world: the Hundred Years War, the Black Plague and even a mini Ice Age (mid-fourteenth century). But then, when all hope was waning, a new wind began to blow: the Renaissance. It brought a resurgence of classical learning with the rediscovery of Aristotle, Plato and Greek thought. The arts were reborn and a new, optimistic humanism replaced the pessimism of the dark times. The Renaissance was like springtime to the West. But the downside was the move to exalt humankind and slowly relegate God to the past.

As humanism was emerging, the church was mired in tedious scholarship. Church leaders focused more on writing complex theology for the educated elite than on making God plain to the masses. But, as in the Middle Ages, God's light would not be extinguished. A bright star was about to burst in the cultural skies: the Reformation.

A.D. 1500-1700

Larsen aptly quotes theologian Francis Schaeffer concerning the birth of the Reformation: "At its core, therefore, the Reformation was the removing of the humanistic distortions which had entered the church."[15] Luther's study of the Scriptures, with special attention given to Romans and Galatians, brought him to his theological breakthrough, sparking the revolution. With the Scriptures as authoritative and central (*sola Scriptura*—only the Bible), he developed the three corollary and freeing truths: *solo Christo*—only Christ; *sola gratia*—only grace; *sola fide*—only faith. Luther would write, "Hence, true faith in Christ is a treasure beyond comparison, which brings with it all salvation and saves from every evil." His preaching was Christ-centered—"Nothing except Christ is to be preached."[16] This truth was welcome after the intellectual meandering of the end of the Middle Ages, which had lost the wonder and experience of conversion in favor of analysis. Calvin, Zwingli and others followed with faithful preaching centered on Christ and derived almost solely from the Scriptures. John Knox sought the salvation of Scotland with his preaching: "He preached with fire and power, alarming sermons, convicting sermons, humbling sermons, converting sermons, and the face of Scotland was changed."[17]

May God raise up an assembly of Luthers, Calvins and Zwinglis in our time. Every age requires thoughtful evangelists and preachers who fight in the marketplace of ideas for God's truth. Recently I (Lon) visited Zurich, Switzerland, with my daughter. It is a big beautiful city, the center of commerce for Switzerland and a major banking center for Europe and the world. The buildings and stores display wealth. In the center of the city we came upon a church, with a statue of Zwingli in front. At one time this church was probably the center of life in Zurich. Today you would miss it if you weren't looking for it. The towering buildings of commerce overshadow it. Urban sociology teaches that a society's values are displayed in the most prominent of its architecture. If Zurich is any example, it teaches us that we must reevangelize Europe.

Even the Reformation's fire dimmed with time. It had been a revival of biblical truth, but soon the political climate of the West and Protestant infighting sucked some of the spiritual life out of the movement. Nations aligned as Protestant or Catholic, Reformed, Anglican or Lutheran. Hatred and fear of the expansionist Turks (Islamic civilization) led people away from the spiritual to geopolitical associations. The fervor for evangelistic activity drained away, until God would ordain the next era of renewal. A glad, powerful, multicontinental awakening was at hand.

THE AWAKENINGS (1700-1850)

Count Zinzendorf wrote on the Moravian Revival, "Our method in proclaiming salvation is this: To point out to every heart the loving Lamb, who died for our sins, by the preaching of His blood, and of His love unto death, even the death of the cross; never, either in the discourse or in the argument, to digress even for a quarter of an hour from the loving Lamb."[18]

The First Great Awakening. The First Great Awakening brought gospel preaching to the forefront in ways perhaps unparalleled since the apostolic era. The latter decades preceding the Awakening saw Pietistic and Puritan efforts to keep the gospel central in the church. Puritan and Pilgrim missionary passion helped plant seeds of truth in the American colonies. According to Dr. John Akers, Puritans placed great emphasis on preaching and on an individual's personal response to God's Word. Evidence of new life in Christ, including repentance and faith, were necessary for church membership.[19] An evangelistic passion evidenced itself in a call to world missions.

Although many colonists were prejudiced against the Native American populations, many who were not started evangelizing them. Some of the more outstanding of these preachers were French Catholic missionary Jacques Marquette and Protestants Thomas Mayhew and John Eliot. Eliot was fairly successful. By 1675, twenty-five hundred—some 20 percent of the Native American population in the New England area—were converted. Eliot organized a translation of the Bible into a dialect of Algonquin. This was the first Bible printed in America (1663). He also ordained some Native American ministers.[20]

In the early 1700s, England, Europe and Colonial America were in spiritual decline again. This period of European and American expansion resulted in economic prosperity, or at least the desire for it. American preacher Cotton Mather lamented, "Religion brought forth prosperity and the daughter destroyed the mother."[21] It was in this climate that the Awakening struck with stunning power. The preaching of Jonathan Edwards, the Mathers and Gilbert Tennent in the colonies, and the Wesleyan revivals in England—spurred by the faithful witness of Moravians to John and Charles Wesley—were the impetus of regeneration. The trumpetlike voice of the once actor, now evangelist George Whitefield thundered on both sides of the Atlantic. Speaking without notes, he proclaimed Christ to crowds as large as twenty thousand. So pervasive was the Awakening in New England that Benjamin Franklin wrote, "It was wonderful to see the change in the manners of our inhabitants. From being thoughtless or indifferent about religion, it seemed as if all the world were growing religious, so that one could not walk thro' the town in an evening without hearing the psalms sung in different families of every street."[22]

As is the case with true revival, social dimensions of life were positively affected. The Awakening led to the abolition of slavery in England under the leadership of evangelical Parliament member William Wilberforce, with help from the Wesleys and their movement. In the colonies, ministry to the Native Americans was undertaken, as previously mentioned. Colleges and other institutions began with Christocentric purposes. The Awakening flowed through the New England colonies, England, Scotland and Wales and continued in other parts of Europe through the Moravian and Pietistic churches and their proclaimers.

The Second Great Awakening. In 1801 the modern missions movement began as leaders such as William Carey and Andrew Sutcliffe dreamed of ways to take the gospel to foreign lands. At the same time, the infant American nation was again in the midst of spiritual decline. Yale President Timothy Dwight declared that the American Revolution "unhinged the principles, the morality, and the religion of the country." By some estimates, less than 10 percent of the population were active church members.[23]

The Second Great Awakening was at hand, and this outpouring would be broader geographically than the first, at least in the United States. Called the Frontier Revival, this movement touched the farmlands of the East and the frontiers of the South and near West. This era spawned the camp meeting movement. Camp meetings were generally a week in length, drawing rural families from wide distances for times of refreshment and revival. Lively and emotional evangelistic preaching was the main activity of the meetings. But while the Second Awakening was primarily rural in nature, even the great universities were touched. By 1802, nearly one-third of Yale's students had converted.

Evangelistic preaching was a large part of the Awakening. Circuit riders, such as Francis Asbury and Peter Cartwright, traveled the trails of the land, proclaiming Christ on every occasion. Asbury was John Wesley's representative in America. In 1771 there were only three hundred Methodists in the land. By 1816, numbers exceeded two hundred thousand. Cartwright traveled by horse for seventy years and was so popular that, at one point, he served in the Illinois legislature. The opponent he defeated for his seat was none other than Abraham Lincoln.

Evangelists were not just white men. Richard Allen, an African American, was a well-respected evangelist who helped found the African Methodist Episcopal Church in 1816 and was the young denomination's first bishop. Sojourner Truth was a black woman who preached Christ and wrote on the situation of slavery. She was preceded by the poet Phyllis Wheatley, a slave in Boston, who wrote on issues "religious and moral" as early as 1773.[24] Phoebe Palmer was a preacher, teacher and author who spoke at hundreds of meetings across the United States, Canada and Great Britain for thirty-seven years, spanning the end of the Second Awakening and into the post-Civil War period. While her theme was primarily the call to the holiness of the saints, she understood the necessity of the new birth. More than twenty thousand were "justified" in her meetings.[25] Palmer was also an activist, serving the social needs of New York City through food, clothing and medical programs. She started schools for the children of poor families and labored for safe workplaces for women.

Undoubtedly the most well-known evangelist of the latter period of the Awakening was Charles Finney. His influence was as profound as Whitefield's, almost a century earlier. Trained as a lawyer, Finney brought razor-sharp logic to his preaching of the gospel. But his influence was broader than gospel speech. He developed many methods of organization that would guide mass campaigns for decades to come. He was a "thoughtful" evangelist who valued education and taught theology, among other things, at Oberlin College during the last forty years of his life. Like all the great evangelists, Finney held strong views on social need. Committed to the abolition of slavery, from Oberlin he would write and speak on its evils. Professors at other colleges, notably Wheaton in Illinois, would follow the pattern. It is quite correct to say that the moral arguments against slavery were fashioned and fired through the biblical theology preached in the Second Awakening in the United States, as they were similarly designed in England during the First Awakening.

URBAN AWAKENING (1850-1900)

As the Second Awakening focused on the rural areas of the United States, the next movement would be centered on cities. William and Catherine Booth launched a joint evangelistic ministry in the 1860s in the cities of England. Both of them preached the gospel with power, calling the lost to Jesus and calling the saved to reach more of the lost. Catherine once declared,

> We should build churches and chapels; but do you think . . . we should rest in this, when three parts of the population utterly ignore our invitations and take no notice whatever of our buildings and of our services? They will not come to us. That is an established fact. What is to be done? They have souls. You profess to believe that as much as I do, and that they must live forever. Where are they going? What is to be done? Jesus Christ says, "go after them."[26]

Her call is as vital for us today as it was in the late nineteenth century. By 1878, the Booths' ministry was formalized and became what we know as the Salvation Army. As they preached in the great cities, they understood the value of the human soul and the body, blending ministry to both with seamless beauty and Christlike passion.

In the United States the YMCA practiced a similar passion and practice. In Chicago, a young believer named Dwight L. Moody began his career teaching a Sunday school class to urban and needy boys. Though only moderately educated, Moody had powerful communication abilities and was able to make the gospel clear and compelling to average people. In 1872, after a consuming encounter with the Holy Spirit, Moody went to England to preach. Twenty-seven months later, the country had been touched in ways similar to those in the Wesley and Whitefield days.

Moody returned to America as the world's most famous evangelist. By the end of his life he had preached to more than 100 million people. But Moody had another passion too. He sought to discover and develop the next generation of Christian leaders and evangelists. His legacy in that regard is still maintained by Moody Bible Institute in Chicago. As the twentieth century emerged, Moody's eye for the next generation of leaders paid rich dividends in the propagation of the gospel of Christ.

THE EARLY TWENTIETH CENTURY

In 1888 Moody conducted a national student conference for 250 select Christian leaders from American colleges and universities. It was his hope that from this conference some of America's brightest and best would sense the call to bring Christ to the great cities of the land. God had a better plan. By the time the conference concluded, more than one hundred of the attendees had made a commitment to take the gospel, not to the nation, but to the world. The Student Volunteer Movement (SVM) had begun, led by student leaders such as John R. Mott and Robert Speers. The "Mount Hermon 100" were the first fruits of a movement that would send more than twenty thousand to the fields of the world within the first few decades of the twentieth century.

Students of other nations caught wind of the SVM and started similar works in their countries. This birthed the World Christian Student Federation, which led to the great world mission conference in Edinburgh in 1910. Evangelist-leader Mott gave direction to these movements through his position with the YMCA's international committee. The Christian youth of the world were on fire to take the gospel to "the uttermost parts."

The other major development of the early-twentieth century was the advent of the Pentecostal movement. With an exuberance for Christ and expanding theology of the Holy Spirit, this movement grew like a forest fire. One evangelist carried the message of Christ and the Holy Spirit like none other. Aimee Semple McPherson saw the gospel as "the ultimate story, a timeless powerful fundamental drama."[27] She had profound understandings of common people and their longings. Her early faith was forged in Salvation Army settings at the time when Evangeline Booth led the movement. With an ongoing commitment to the soul and the body, Salvation Army disciples understood the deep realities of human pain. Undoubtedly the years with them also taught McPherson that God used women as well as men to proclaim the gospel.

Centered in Los Angeles where McPherson began her church, the Angelus Temple, she proclaimed Christ and practiced prayer for healing. With a flair for the dramatic, she and her staff publicized the spiritual and physical healings occurring in the church. From there, she traveled extensively. More were converted through her ministry than that of Billy Sunday (who we will discuss later). The International Church of the Four Square Gospel, which today has a large and growing mission throughout the world, emerged from her ministry. In 1927 McPherson stated, "It is so simple, so very simple. Believing the story of Jesus, believing that the way to salvation is only through Him . . . I have been compelled by my faith and belief for eighteen years to send the message of His undying love from the pulpit, in tent, tabernacle and over the radio to every ear that could be induced to listen."[28] While some questionable practices surrounded her life and ministry, there is no denying she was mightily used of God during an important era in the history of the church.

Another notable, but sometimes overlooked, evangelist of the early twentieth century was Wilbur Chapman. He is overlooked because he bridged the eras of Moody, McPherson and Sunday. Unlike those three, Chapman was highly educated. He wrote thirty books and also served five churches as a pastor before moving to itinerant evangelism, giving him a deep respect for the pastor and the local church. He understood that the role of the evangelist was to work with the church to save the lost. Thus he held special programs in addition to his main large-group meetings, reaching shut-ins, the elderly, the poor and other specialized groups who would not normally attend big events. Chapman utilized other evangelists in his larger city meetings as well. It was the practice to have several of these "simultaneous campaigns" occurring in different parts of a city at the same time. These ideas were very successful. The campaign in Philadelphia in the spring of 1908 had a total attendance of 1.4 million.[29] A New York reporter summarized Chapman's style and substance:

> The end of the godless, the torture and horror of hell seemed not half so great as the sweetness of the grace and love of God. A stillness that was impressive came over the auditorium as he rose to speak; tall and sturdy, he leaned forward over the pulpit and began. Here was no passion, no loudness in his voice, but it reached to every corner. It was as if he were a father pleading with his children.[30]

Billy Sunday was a professional baseball player who came to Christ through the ministry of the Pacific Garden Mission in Chicago. Like McPherson, Sunday's personality was larger than life. He was discipled by Chapman and served on his staff before entering his own itinerant career. By 1910, after fifteen years of holding small meetings in the rural Midwest, he entered the arenas of America's big cities. His campaigns used specially designed wooden tabernacles that held more than five thousand people.

Sunday attacked the social demise of America, particularly alcoholism, and urged people to repent and come to Christ. He also waved the patriotic flag of America with vigor. Critics rightly assess that Sunday focused too much on a pro-American agenda. Because much of his ministry occurred during and after World War I, this is understandable. But let all evangelists learn from this, remembering that the core of our message is Jesus Christ and him crucified. Our kingdom is the kingdom of God, and it has no national or geographical borders. To Sunday's credit, millions heard the gospel. By the end of his career, untold numbers had walked the sawdust trail, born anew.

Communications technology advanced in this era too. In 1923 Pastor Paul Rader was preaching weekly over Chicago's first radio station. Walter Maier, a Lutheran seminary professor, started the *Lutheran Hour* broadcast. McPherson started California's third radio station, and by 1932 had established a network of missionary stations.[31]

But all was not well. Akers points out that growing theological controversies between modernists and fundamentalists polarized the American church and hindered wide-scale evangelistic pursuits. The effects of these controversies can still be felt in parts of the church today.

NEW MOVEMENTS (1950-2000)

The last half of the twentieth century witnessed the emergence of the parachurch movement in the church of the United States and other parts of the world. Ministries such as Youth for Christ, under evangelist Torrey Johnson's visionary leadership; InterVarsity Christian Fellowship, with impressive evangelists and apologists; Young Life; Campus Crusade; Youth With A Mission and others provided fresh energy and ideas for evangelism. Each movement considered evangelistic preaching a core component of its efforts.

Billy Graham emerged in this era as well. Serving first with Youth For Christ, he developed a powerful speaking style that reached youth as well as adults. His insights into the demise of Western culture and the effects of sin on individuals and societies opened doors for his message throughout the world. Not much needs to be said of Graham in this brief chapter on the history of evangelistic preaching because of the rich plethora of materials available. Suffice it to say, he has proclaimed Christ to more people than any other person in history.

Graham's profound leadership gift is often overlooked. Like Mott in the era before him, Graham had the vision, energy and passion to bring the evangelical world together numerous times in international conferences to reawaken the church to the centrality of evangelism. His commitment to scholarship is also quite impressive, evidenced by his founding of *Christianity Today,* his major role in starting Gordon-Conwell Theological Seminary and, of course, his legacy in the Billy Graham Center at Wheaton College. With equal access to kings and commoners, Graham is a man for the ages.

The fast growth of the Pentecostal and charismatic movements throughout the world continued in this era. Millions claimed Christ as a result of the faithful, Spirit-filled witness of this wing of the church. Like Graham in the evangelical arm of the church, a notable evangelist couple emerged in the Pentecostal church. Tommy Lee (T. L.) and Daisy Osborn began their ministry in the mountains of Oklahoma in 1941. Within a decade God had opened a global ministry of evangelism and healing. By 1953 the Osborns witnessed more than one hundred thousand decisions for Christ in the Caribbean and Central America alone. Evangelistic missions throughout Africa and Asia, as well as the United States, yielded countless numbers of faith decisions.

Today the Osborn Foundation maintains headquarters in Tulsa, Oklahoma, with international branches in major cities throughout the world. Their literature and media ministry publishes in more than eighty languages. Their commitment to the gospel that heals the soul and the body, combined with the leadership to provide nationals with training in church planting, was—and is—exemplary.[32]

Both evangelical and Pentecostal/charismatic movements span the world, with a driving desire to see people saved and brought to the knowledge of Jesus Christ.

WHAT'S NEXT? (2000-?)

There we have it. A breathtaking but oh-so-short and incomplete view of gospel speech through the ages. The God who "was pleased through the foolishness of what was preached to save those who believe" (1 Cor 1:21) continues unabated in his passionate, loving quest for souls.

Our prayer is that some readers of this book will take up the mantle in ways unimagined. God is a creative God. Let us be convinced, however, that the prayerful, faithful proclamation of the gospel of Jesus Christ will be a sail on the winds of God's Spirit.

PART 2

WHAT HAPPENED TO EVANGELISTIC PREACHING?

5

THE CASE OF THE
MISSING EVANGELIST

To this point, we've tried to make a case for going public with the gospel. We've mentioned that this special evangelism role has suffered neglect in the last couple of decades. The next two chapters suggest why.

Evangelists are a rare breed of Christian. Researcher George Barna reported in 2001 through the monthly *Barna Report* that only 8 percent of clergy feel they possess the gift of the evangelist. The figure among the laity is even smaller. Why is this? Has God been stingy in dispersing this seemingly vital gift, or is there something else at play?

In informal surveys of church members taken throughout the 1990s, people were asked to describe an evangelist. Evangelists were seen primarily in two categories. The first could be labeled "Someone I wouldn't want to be." It included adjectives such as loud, brash, Bible thumping, obnoxious, puffy haired, immoral, yelling, tent dwelling, money hungry, male only and the like. Such descriptions are promoted by Hollywood, with movies like Steve Martin's *Leap of Faith*, whose lead character became the 1990s version of Sinclair Lewis's fallen cleric, Elmer Gantry. But blaming a culture determined to undermine God's messengers in the media won't cut it. The fall of notable Christian leaders in the last two decades reinforces the perception of the Gantryesque evangelist. And remember, the survey was of church members.

The other category of responses to the "What is an evangelist?" question covers the other extreme, which we call, "Something so great I could never attain it." It is described using adjectives such as charismatic, Bible expert, powerful, winsome, caring, convincing. When asked to give the first words that come to mind upon hearing the word *evangelist*, the answer was almost always "Billy Graham."

I (Lon) labored under both perceptions for years. People would tell me I was an evangelist and I would first shudder and then laugh. I did not want to be perceived as an Elmer Gantry and I knew I was no Billy Graham. While my heart yearned for the lost and I had a special intuitive capacity to speak to seeking people, I knew I was a minor leaguer compared to the Billy Grahams, Bill Brights and Leighton Fords of the world. Further, my calling at that time was to the local church, and I didn't know evangelists are called more often to local settings than to itinerant ministry. I was a communicator of the gospel, but I did not see myself as an evangelist.

It doesn't take much to see that either of the above two perceptions leaves the church without the office of the evangelist operating effectively. According to these perceptions, evangelists are either so corrupt no one in his or her right mind would choose to become one, or they are so lofty that to aspire to such is the epitome of arrogance. This explains in part why there are so few evangelists. But there's an even bigger reason.

The perception in the United States has been that we are a Christian nation, and therefore the role of the evangelist is not required. There are no more Whitefields or McPhersons because there doesn't need to be. The West is won, or so the saying goes. Thankfully the church-growth movement in the 1980s unmasked this assumption at least to some degree. The West, including North America and Europe, is post-Christian at best. Vast populations are either unaware of the Christian gospel or clearly rejecting it in favor of other worldviews. Missiologists since the 1970s write of the billions without Christ in the "closed" or "avoided" regions commonly called the 10/40 Window.

We contend that the need for the proclamation evangelist, or public proclaimer, has never been greater in our world. A large army of "heralds" is required to place the greatest of all ideas—the gospel of Christ—at the forefront of thought for every human being. "Go ye therefore" has never been as necessary as today.

When the apostle Paul described the organizational plan of Christ's body, the church, he stated the necessity of at least four—and probably five—key offices functioning in the strategic leadership structure (depending on how you read the pastor-teacher language in the text). Apostles, prophets, pastors, teachers and evangelists were to Paul the essential gifts to the church for building up the saints (see Eph 4:11-12).

The gift of the apostle and that of the prophet are defined somewhat differently by evangelicals, depending on theological perspectives. The apostle then and now has some level of governance over the body. While some see the apostle as the starter of new missions and works, in today's world it seems the apostle is more an overseer of a ministry organization or group of churches. These may be agency leaders, denominational executives and so on. They do see the extension of the church as important for reaching the lost, but are more exercised to organize the church as a growing, engaging army that then reaches out.

Prophets provide clear direction for the body. They see clearly the difference between light and dark, and they call the church to obedience and purity. While the apostle operates outside a single local church, the prophet may be located inside or outside the local fellowship. Chuck Colson is a leading prophet for the church today; he has a brilliant ability to diagnose culture and mission and to call the church to action. This, too, is a gift primarily, though not exclusively, for the body.

The pastor provides oversight, care and leadership to a local congregation. For the long-term health of the church, the pastor may be the most important office. The teacher instructs the church in the Scriptures and brings application for life today. Teachers are essential for all aspects of the life of faith and are needed for every category of Christ follower, whether young children of faith or seminary students. Today we place high value on the gifts of pastor and teacher, and rightly so. Without the pastoral office and gift, the church would lack compassion and grace-filled caring. Without the teacher gift, we would lack clear understanding of the Scriptures and the theology of the Christian faith. No church structure thrives without both offices in operation.

THE EVANGELIST

The offices/gifts mentioned above exist primarily for the church and guide the church. But there's one more: the evangelist. Like the others, this gift is essential for the health of the body, but its focus is beyond the church. The evangelist stretches the church beyond itself. He or she reminds the church of its essential mission to seek out and save the lost. While the other offices function primarily for the body of believers, the evangelist has an eye and a passionate heart for the "yet to be born." When the evangelistic gift and office operate effectively, the church moves to evangelize. This preparation occurs through motivation, teaching and, quite often, strategic planning. How does an evangelist carry out the office? We suggest several ways.

Models an evangelistic lifestyle. First, the evangelist motivates and teaches the church to evangelize by modeling an evangelistic lifestyle. This means the evangelist seeks to reach people through his or her own network of relationships. Personal evangelism is the best way for most Christians to share their faith. So, too, for the evangelist. Like every believer, the evangelist must be praying for lost neighbors, friends and family, and trying to find open doors to tell them the good news about Christ.

Trains the church in evangelism. Second, from such a lifestyle the evangelist can then teach the church the "art" of evangelizing. How wonderful it would be if every evangelist, especially those called to the work of the itinerant, also had a ministry of leading evangelism in a local church. Whether in a paid staff position or not, the evangelist would greatly help the pastors and teachers equip the saints to be missionaries in their own neighborhoods and workplaces.

We suggest that some form of personal evangelism training be a core component of every local church's teaching cycle. Let your evangelists conduct the classes. Why? Because the person in the office of the evangelist will, by nature, focus in two ways: personally reaching the lost, and encouraging and motivating the church to do the same. It should also be pointed out that even evangelists who travel more than they operate out of the local church are teachers of evangelism. No campaign in a town, city or local church will be successful if the evangelist or someone in his or her organization does not provide excellent personal evangelism training to the churches involved. For it is God's people who pray and invite pre-Christians to hear the gospel. Evangelist Steve Wingfield says that mass evangelism "is only personal evangelism done in a mass evangelism setting." Thus teaching evangelism is central to the calling of all evangelists.

Looks for emerging evangelists. The third aspect of the evangelist's job description is to look for believers with the same gift and help them reach their potential in evangelism. At a prayer meeting during a Billy Graham mission, one intercessor prayed for a thousand Billy Grahams to be raised up by God. The evangelist is always looking for those with the passion and God-given ability to extend the work. If mature and willing to share the spotlight, such evangelists will do far more by mentoring other evangelists than they will through their own preaching and personal witness.

Another organization deeply committed to raising up evangelists is the Luis Palau Evangelistic Association. Through its Next Generation Alliance, the Palau team, led by Dr. Tim Robnett and Executive Vice President Kevin Palau, is devoted to discovering, developing and networking emerging evangelists into the church worldwide.

Proclaims Christ publicly. Finally, the office of the evangelist brings the gift of public proclamation to the forefront. Not all persons with the gift of evangelism are also gifted public communicators. But those who are, are privileged to enter the arena of public proclamation. The evangelist must work diligently to build his or her speaking skills, while at the same time being a student of the Scriptures and the culture. Some preaching evangelists will be stronger at personal evangelism than at proclamation. This is as it should be, for they can best model and teach the church to do the same.

But many will possess both abilities—and how we need them!

The proclaimer has been given an awesome responsibility by God: "If anyone speaks, he should do it as one speaking the very words of God"(1 Pet 4:11). The only way to speak the words of God is first to be so close to God that we hear his voice. The second is to so know the Word of God that we can proclaim its truth with clarity to every culture and generation. Those called to proclaim the gospel are under a divine compulsion (see 1 Cor 9:16). It is our prayer that seminaries, Bible colleges and ministry training centers will see the task of training leaders to preach to pre-Christian people as important to the church. After all, there are billions of people on the planet who will not "hear without someone preaching to them" (Rom 10:14).

Thus the office of evangelist contains at least four assignments. First, to do personal evangelism; second, to equip the church for the work of evangelism; third, to raise up and mentor other leaders with the gift of evangelism and finally, to proclaim Christ publicly.

OVERCOMING BAD PRESS

Proclamation evangelism is a mighty ministry in the body of Christ. Perhaps that is why this form of evangelism has been in the church since Peter's first message in Jerusalem. The gospel of Jesus Christ is an idea. The proclaimer hurls the gospel idea into the culture. There the gospel does its work of dividing truth from error by placing biblical wisdom into many aspects of human existence. When Paul preached in the marketplace of Athens, his words and concepts caught wings and flew into the prevailing philosophies of the day. Soon he was on Mars Hill, presenting Christ to leading thinkers of the day. The gospel is a *living* message. Like a good virus, it infects the worldview. Like a good vaccine, it heals a culture.

Recently the Billy Graham Center at Wheaton College conducted a meeting with several prominent public proclaimers. Almost all present spoke of how difficult it is to get invitations for mass evangelism meetings. If mass evangelism has so much going for it, why are so few communities utilizing it as an evangelism method? Certainly any community or group of churches entertaining thoughts of a campaign knows the preparation is arduous. Preparation phases require anywhere from six months for single-church campaigns to more than a year for citywide gatherings. Steve Wingfield of Wingfield Encounters and Kevin Palau, executive vice president of the Luis Palau Evangelistic Association (BGEA), said that mass evangelism meetings are perceived as ineffective, in part because of a widely read and quoted article somewhat critical of Graham's Seattle Campaign of 1976.

The power of one negative voice is amazing. It takes at least five positive voices to counterbalance one negative voice. Perceptions, whether true or false, take on a life of their own after a time. In this case, twenty-five years after the article, the perception has become truth to many Christian leaders, especially in the West.

The article in question was written by Dr. Win Arn of the American Church Growth Institute in the January/February 1978 issue of *Church Growth Magazine*. In the article, Arn evaluated the results of a study of 1,200 pastors interviewed one year after participating in the Seattle campaign. Essentially the study concluded that of the 18,136 decisions recorded, only 15.3 percent became members of local churches. I (Lon) remember the effect of this data. Sadly I, like many other devotees of the heady new science of church growth, used this data as proof positive that mass evangelism was at best passé and certainly ineffectual. Further, Arn found that only 30.6 percent of the decisions were "conversion." More than 53 percent were rededications, and it was unclear what type of decision was made by nearly 16 percent. From this he discerned that the Seattle campaign was more mass revival than mass evangelism.

To his credit, Arn did not malign mass evangelism in his article. That was left to others reacting to his data. Rather he argued for some ways to increase the value of campaign evangelism. Perhaps the most valuable discovery in the study was that 83 percent of those who made decisions at the campaign and became members of a congregation were linked to the congregation by an existing relationship with a friend, family member or other person. Sterling Huston, former director of North American Crusades for

BGEA, believes that between 80 and 90 percent of attendees link their attendance to the "invite" from a relational link. This concept of friends bringing friends has always been foundational in the Graham strategy.

In 1979 the Billy Graham Evangelistic Association asked Vanderbilt sociologist Glenn Firebaugh to conduct a study of the same mission, using a larger and more diverse sample. Graham scholar and researcher Robert Ferm had earlier found the numbers of unchurched persons making decisions at missions to be in the range of 46 percent.[1] But the Firebaugh work expanded on Ferm's findings, and *Christianity Today* published the results in May 1981. Essentially the Firebaugh study concluded that the Seattle campaign had a very positive effect on the church in greater Seattle. Firebaugh challenged Arn's new-member figures, stating they were off by five hundred persons, placing the actual percentage of church membership at more than 18 percent.

More importantly, he questioned Arn's evaluative norm. To Arn, *church membership* was the only criterion of success. Firebaugh argued that perhaps other measurements were required. What about using increased church attendance as a measurement? After all, Arn's study was conducted only one year after the mission. Many converts were probably still in the early stages of discipleship and had not yet joined local congregations. If attendance had been used rather than membership, the number would have been much higher. Further, Arn's study did not allow for converts who may have joined a congregation other than the one that originated their follow-up. The figures were tallied from calls to the pastors originally assigned to call the inquirers. If an inquirer did not attend, all the interviewees could state was that the inquirer was not involved in their congregation.

The conversion-versus-rededication ratio Arn referenced was essentially correct. Firebaugh's figures stated more than 57 percent of the decisions were recorded as rededications. But he overlooked the possibility that many church attendees and members need to be converted to Christ. Every one of these types of inquirers would have been categorized as "rededication" by the counselors who assisted them. Only God knows exactly what occurs in the heart and mind of someone who makes a public profession for

Christ. We are convinced, however, that many who say they are rededicating, or whose counselor discerns as rededicating, may be making their first definitive decision, even if they attended church most of their lives. Too often, church membership, occasional church attendance, childhood baptism or confirmation, or even good works is the criterion that defines "Christian." In such cases the decision made at a public meeting may be more than the inquirer or the counselor perceives. As someone aptly put it, "I needed to be born again, again."

Most convincingly, Firebaugh interviewed participating pastors as well as participating lay leaders and those who made spiritual decisions. Three years later, all three groups said the effects of the campaign were positive. The inquirers in the study were asked if they would make the decision for Christ again. A full 86 percent said yes.

Finally, Firebaugh's study suggested that those who were involved in the Seattle campaign saw it as very successful for many reasons in addition to new believers being brought into the local churches. They felt the campaign was effective in reviving the local church, in training church members in evangelism and counseling, in raising the spiritual consciousness of the area and in uniting denominations for a single cause.

Unfortunately the good news of Firebaugh's article in 1981 did little to dispel the perceived bad news of 1978. Today hundreds and perhaps thousands of churches and cities in the West dismiss the redemptive value of public evangelism meetings. May God change this direction and do so speedily. Oh, the wonder of God's one church in every city as it collaborates to bring lost and loved people to hear the gospel preached, for "God was pleased through the foolishness of what was preached to save those who believe" (1 Cor 1:21).

OVERCOMING "PRIVATE" FAITH

The demise, or perceived demise, of public proclamation may also relate to a societal shift, at least in the West. We love our privacy as much or more than community. Sociologists point out that modern realities such as television, computers and even home air-conditioners contribute to a withdrawal from "grouping." The front porch has been replaced by climate-controlled family and computer rooms. Individualism probably helps breed such isolation. And individualism's tentacles reach deeply into all areas of life. *My* family, *my* church, *my* team is simply individualism masked as "tight" community. It is harder to get churches to cooperate in area-wide campaigns today. The notion that "it's not *our* way of doing evangelism" hinders much unified effort.

But are people attending fewer mass events (or will they), whether they be county fairs or citywide evangelism campaigns? Let's not assume large-group gatherings are passé. Major musical groups break attendance records every year. As we write, summer films are hitting theaters. Blockbusters abound. More people chose to see films in theaters this year than last, and more last year than the previous year. In fact, movie buffs argue that a good film can't be appreciated unless it is viewed in a theater with strangers all around. The experience is enhanced in community.

Starbucks defies the individualization trend too. These coffee houses are loaded with loners who may or may not speak to each other. And who can explain the attendance at Chicago Cubs games? Why would a chronically losing team draw crowds day in and day out. They don't even have parking lots. Why this "grouping" need? These illustrations, and even the rise of megachurches, suggest something is warring against the isolation.

Perhaps God was right. It wasn't good for Adam to be alone, and it isn't good for us either. Human beings are by nature communal. Something draws us to a crowd. Without a doubt, societies celebrate togetherness, whether it's a Cubs game, a football match, a U2 concert or a New Year's celebration.

Rather than viewing public evangelism as a detriment, the church should see it as a value. Communication theorists know that communication is enhanced in a group, not diminished. So is persuasion. Communication occurs between the sender (speaker) and the receiver (listener), and nonverbally between listener and listener.

Quoting a line from the 1980s film *Field of Dreams*, we believe that when it comes to relevant public evangelism events, if you build it, they will come.

THE BENEFITS OF PROCLAIMING CHRIST PUBLICLY

What are some benefits of the public proclamation of the gospel in community-wide or multiple-church settings? There are at least twelve.

1. It assists the church to be obedient to the Great Commission. As stated in chapter three, it was God's idea to use preaching as a primary means to save lost people (see Lk 24:47; Rom 10:15-17; 1 Cor 1:21). Nothing in life is quite as sweet as sensing we are in the midst of God's redemptive activity. In this work, we work with God (see 1 Cor 3:9).

2. It pulls loose ends together. Good evangelistic preaching does in thirty minutes what months and even years of casual sharing with a person may not accomplish. It pulls together the bits and pieces of information gathered from books, tracts, television, the Internet, radio and conversations with believers. It ties together the loose ends of an inquirer's questions and takes him or her in an orderly way toward a spiritual decision. In a world of multiple messages barking for people's attention and devotion, the herald makes God's life-producing gospel compelling and attractive under the anointing of the Holy Spirit.

3. It enhances the local church's sense of purpose. In the local church setting, there are additional reasons to have a steady diet of evangelistic preaching. As I (Lon) practiced public proclamation in my pastorates, I found the mission of our church as a whole was enhanced. All pastors know how easy it is to say the church evangelizes, but how hard it is to put that into practice. Evangelistic preaching reminds the church of the importance of reaching a lost world. It also trains the church to do evangelism "on the sly." A church chairman once told me that every time I preached the gospel I was giving the church family another lesson on how to share their faith. For a while I gave an invitation each week, and during that time I gave the church multiple ways to tell the story. And here is another wonderful effect of evangelistic preaching on the local church: Each time we present the gospel, the believing congregation is reminded of the mystery and the wonder of what God has done for us in Christ. In a way, it is like looking at old family picture albums. It reminds us of our heritage and of how great it is to be a part of the family of God.

4. It disciples the church. Campaign evangelism has the potential of stirring the church out of lethargy. If 10 percent or more of a local fellowship get involved through praying, inviting friends and neighbors, counseling, ushering or any manner of involvement, it will invigorate the whole church.

Because mass evangelism is merely personal evangelism done on a broader scale, a multichurch or community-wide event includes good training in personal evangelism. All would agree that a discipled believer is one who believes in and is equipped to do personal evangelism. When special training in personal evangelism is conducted by the evangelist's team or the pastors and leaders of the community in conjunction with a public proclamation event, the sense of urgency creates more desire to learn. Because of the campaign's possibilities, believers take new interest in the Scriptures and in ways to help people progress in faith. Thus the whole process of discipleship accelerates. And hopefully the effects of this go far beyond the proclamation event. For many believers who throw themselves into the work of the campaign, new patterns of obedience may result in long-term lifestyle changes.

5. It creates God-consciousness. Proclamation evangelism creates a God-consciousness in a larger community of people. Whether the setting is a small group of churches in a small community or a large number in an urban area, the focus on the Christian message creates a community-wide "spiritual" atmosphere. Prayer saturation has tilled the soil. It becomes easier to talk with people about the Lord. If the event receives media coverage, the result is even more apparent. Inquirers and seeking people are mysteriously drawn not just to the meetings, but to thoughts of God.

6. It permeates the community's institutions and leaders. Well-planned meetings include prayer for and strategic invitations to community leaders. The God-consciousness not only touches the community at large but also reaches influential people in the community. Very often they will attend because community leaders, especially elected officials, understand the importance of a crowd. Suffice it to say, these leaders are strategic contacts in all gospel efforts. They are the powers that be and thus come under the bright light of the gospel. As Bill Bright has wisely said, "All souls are equally precious, but not all souls are equally strategic."

7. *It witnesses through unity.* According to Jesus, nothing gives evidence of him quite as much as the church unified. Whether the events you plan include five churches or five hundred, the effect of witness is multiplied by the beauty of the church unified. Reports from communities holding campaigns show that the unity can have ongoing and wonderful community impact. Denominational lines are crossed and, even more important, local churches start to work together. They share potlucks and prayer meetings. The *churches* of the city become the *church* of the city.

8. *It dislodges the powers of darkness.* There are entrenched forces of darkness that dominate communities and cities. These are broken down when the church, in obedience to the commands of Jesus Christ, moves in a unified way with public proclamation. Prayer certainly assists in the toppling of forces of darkness. Proclamation of Christ and him crucified finishes the task as the gospel attacks the evil values and ideas of a community, heralding the truth in the midst of darkness. It is the proclamation of Christ that "take[s] captive every thought to make it obedient to Christ" (2 Cor 10:5), as we discuss in chapter ten, "Spiritual Warfare."

9. *It shows believers the "bigness" of the church.* Because most churches in America have less than two hundred attendees, Christians seldom see the vastness of God's people. The church gathered is a formidable group in any community. Believers are therefore reminded that they are not alone, that they are part of the world's largest institution. One might ask why the church gathered for a picnic or Christian concert would not accomplish this purpose as well as an evangelistic campaign. The answer is, because, by and large, only believers are involved. In an evangelistic campaign, the church gathers with seeking people, showing not only its size but also its true purpose.

10. *It results in salvation.* Nothing is quite as exciting for believers as wit-

nessing God pour out new life on dying souls. And heaven rejoices. In proclamation events, we sense that our great purpose for living—to seek out and rescue the lost—is being fulfilled. Souls are being rescued from sin and eternal hell. And what is more important? Further, because most of the meetings give an opportunity for some kind of public response (walking forward, filling out cards, raising hands and so on), the inquirer has made a visible step of commitment. Friends, neighbors and coworkers are watching. This can help the inquirer stay in Christ with more fervor than those who make secret decisions.

11. *It creates contagious personal evangelists.* For years we have heard that only a small percentage of believers ever participate with God in leading a person to Christ. Some say the percentage is as low as 5 percent. Whatever the actual figures of those who effectively evangelize, we can be sure that it rises dramatically during a proclamation campaign. Personal sharing before and after the events, combined with the large numbers of believers who counsel seekers during the events, ensures that more believers become harvesters for the rest of their lives. Why? Because once believers witness the new birth, they are addicted.

12. *It glorifies God.* Proclamation evangelism glorifies God because, as Kevin Palau states, it lifts up "the holiness of His name; it exalts the person and work of His Son, and, it communicates God's grace" in the extraordinary story of Jesus. God's heart is pleased when the fragrance of the knowledge of him is so beautifully spread.

Going public with the gospel is one of the unique ways God uses the evangelist in the church. Proclaiming Christ publicly powerfully assists discipleship in the body, and it brings the churches and Christian institutions of a community together, which is evangelistic in itself. Most important, God is glorified as lost people are brought from darkness to life through the faithful prayers and invitations of friends and neighbors combined with the anointed proclamation of the preachers.

6

THE LOST GOSPEL

In the last chapter we tried to show the value and define the roles of the evangelist and of public proclamation. But there is a problem: To some extent, we have lost the gospel. Have we made conversion so easy and the requirements so few that many inquirers miss the real thing? Could it be that we've caught the climate of this world's values and philosophies in our evangelism?

King Herod had John the Baptist arrested because John confronted his sin by rebuking him for living in adultery with his sister-in-law. Eventually the king ordered John beheaded. Jesus had the highest regard for John. He said, "Among those born of women there has not risen anyone greater than John the Baptist" (Mt 11:11). John's message can be defined in one word: *repent!* The ideas of sin and repentance have been largely lost in our time. They are among the many missing elements in much modern preaching.

THE EARLY DAYS OF OUR LIFE WITH CHRIST

In the years before we married, my wife, Karen, and I (Mark) were dramatically changed as a result of the Jesus Movement. These were the days of preachers like Keith Green and Leonard Ravenhill who were firebrand revivalists calling us to complete surrender to Jesus. Pleasing God was the goal no matter what the cost. Holiness and complete separation unto God was required—not optional. Salvation was a decision born out of a deep conviction of our sinfulness. We went to the altar to ask for God's mercy because of preaching that brought the fear of the Lord. We knew we were lost, going to hell and desperately in need of the Savior. Jesus was asking us to recognize and renounce our sin. Our whole way of life had to change. We came to the altar for a new life because we knew we needed one.

Responding to this kind of preaching, my wife and I were radically saved and filled with the Spirit, and we began to serve the Lord fully. We were affected in every area of our lives, committing our relationship, our careers, our future family and our money to God. For us, the most important question of daily life was, "Lord, what is your will?" For hours every week, we searched the Scriptures to find out how God wanted us to live. We discovered that the primary mandate of Jesus was to go and make disciples of all nations, so that is exactly what we began to do. We made lists of our relatives and friends who didn't know the Lord, then developed strategies to reach each one, praying for them every day. In the first year after surrendering everything to Jesus, we led thirty-two people to Christ.

THE COST-NOTHING GOSPEL

Before being changed by the message preached in the Jesus Movement, we both had grown up as church kids. I was a nominal Lutheran, and Karen was an evangelical. But we hadn't been living for God.

Karen grew up in a Christian home and attended a large evangelical church, one of the largest in the nation. The church leaders were committed and sincere in their love for Jesus. Karen made a decision for Christ in her fourth-grade Sunday school class. For the next few years she was a "good Christian girl." All this changed in the latter part of her seventh-grade year. Worldly influences finally wore down her spiritual values. She continued to attend youth group and Sunday services and was even on the Bible quiz team. But she wasn't living for God. Neither were most of her friends. They were all in the youth group but seemed to have little fear of the Lord.

Karen and I grew up less than a mile from each other, attended the same schools and had mutual friends. I remember seeing some of the kids from her youth group at weekend parties; they were often the rowdiest, most rebellious kids there. It struck me as very odd that they were involved so much in church but behaved as they did. I wasn't a Christian at the time and knew very little about the Bible, but I still had a sense of right and wrong. Somehow this seemed to be missing in many of these church kids. Why?

The influence of humanism. I believe there are two primary reasons. First, the world's influence is often stronger than that of the church. In the latter part of the nineteenth century, under progressives like John Dewey, schools became instruments for social transformation. Entirely new sets of educational premises were implemented. These premises were sociological and psychological in nature. Curriculum strayed from the traditional arithmetic, science, reading and writing.

These influences come from various forms of humanism departing from Judeo-Christian values. Secular humanism (atheistic) was promoted by the Humanist Manifestos I & II of 1933 and 1973. Cosmic humanism (pantheistic) was popularized through the writings of philosophers such as Spangler and Ferguson. These worldviews go back to the teachings of the ancient Greek and Roman cultures—pagan societies consumed with hedonism, where everything was defined by the pursuit of pleasure and immediate gratification, where sacrifice and pain were to be avoided. These forms of humanism define everything from a human perspective, leaving God out. In some cases, God is even in the way.

These views dominate the Western world in our time. In reality, a form of humanism is our religion, practiced in our educational systems and supported by our media. And it has become the unofficial but prevailing theology in much of the Western evangelical church.

Growing up and studying in secular schools for twelve years, thirty-three hours a week, we received instruction without biblical foundations. In junior high and high school much of the instruction contradicted the Bible. Much of the teaching was anti-Christian, steeped in evolution, relativism and self-actualization, and void of moral absolutes. Day after day we were taught that self-gratification and personal happiness were the highest goals. The concept of anything being sinful was ridiculed, considered a throwback to Puritan ideals left over from the seventeenth century. Nothing was absolute except that there are no absolutes, only opinions. The highest ideal we were taught was tolerance. Added to this was the peer pressure to fit in by drinking, doing drugs, having sex and taking foolish risks. It was almost impossible to live a holy life.

Even so, I have a deep respect for the many dedicated Christians who serve as teachers, principals and superintendents in our public schools. Before my older brother, Bruce, went to be with the Lord, he worked with junior high students and was a guide for many troubled youths. He confided in me that he was concerned about the deteriorating moral environment of modern education. These teachers and school leaders need our prayer. They are our missionaries to children and young adults and play a key role in shaping their future.

It's all about me. The second reason Karen and her friends were not living for God, in spite of all their church activities, was the language they heard defining what it meant to be a Christian. People in past generations grew up in a nation that respected Christian ideals and had a basic fear of the Lord. Even the voices in education and media were usually rooted in Christian values. To this older generation, terms used by ministers, such as "accepting Christ," "asking Christ into your heart" or "trusting in Christ" made sense. This is no longer the case for emerging generations.

If you tell average people today, who are saturated in a secular worldview, to accept Christ into their hearts or to trust Christ to receive salvation, they will. But they have no intention of changing how they live. If you say, "God loves you and has a plan for your life," they think, "Of course God loves me; life is about me." Those living in a predominantly secular world have little understanding of God as their creator or of the fall of humanity and the subsequent judgment. In their minds, they are simply accepting an offer for a free pass to heaven. Preaching that salvation is a free gift is the worst thing to tell a generation that already believes they deserve every good thing without paying a price.

I was startled a few years ago after reading a George Barna survey that said 82 percent of Americans think they are born again and 90 percent believe they are going to heaven. Yet most people, including many evangelicals, say they do not believe in hell. How can this be?

After all our years of evangelistic ministry, we believe the quality of the decision for Christ largely determines what kind of Christians people will become. I speak with frustrated church leaders all the time who complain about the lack of commitment of their church members, who are unwilling to serve or give their time.

While many factors create this problem, the largest one could be how people define Christianity. Many were told at the time of their decision, "God loves you and has a wonderful plan for your life. He wants to bless you and give you the desires of your heart. All of this is free and costs you nothing." Then they are asked to pray a simple prayer, asking Christ into their hearts. After the prayer they are told, "Your sins have been forgiven and you are on your way to heaven." Why should these people live righteously? They have accepted a cost-nothing gospel, which is not the gospel at all. It is really only "simply believe and you're in." This isn't what Jesus taught or what the disciples practiced. Salvation is free in the sense that we can't earn it by our good works, but inquirers must understand it will cost them everything. Contrast how typical Western churchgoers live with the lifestyle of the disciples who left everything to follow Jesus. It could not be more different.

FOLLOWING JESUS

How did Jesus define what it means to be a Christian? Of course, he did not use the term *Christian*. He used the terms *follower* or *disciple*. These are much more meaningful and definitive.

After Jesus was baptized, he began to call his disciples. This is recorded for us in Matthew 4: "As Jesus was walking beside the Sea of Galilee, he saw two brothers, Simon called Peter and his brother Andrew. They were casting a net into the lake, for they were fishermen. 'Come, follow me,' Jesus said, 'and I will make you fishers of men.' At once they left their nets and followed him" (vv. 18-20). What an amazing response! They gave up their careers for their faith.

Jesus used the simple phrase "Come, follow me." In these words, he gave us the framework for true Christianity—a simple but profound idea: become a follower of Jesus. Most people who call themselves Christians in the Western world do not see themselves as followers of Jesus. They speak of believing in God or adding Christ to their lives as a kind of eternal insurance. Many see God as a benevolent Buddha whose job is to make them happy and give them stuff. Their framework follows their secular worldview: I am what life is about. The primary objective in life is to be happy. Why shouldn't they think this? That is what they were told when they made their decision, and too often it is reinforced by much of our instruction.

THE EXCHANGED LIFE

During the 1970s and 1980s I watched the gospel that was preached deteriorate into a self-serving, self-help philosophy. Modern psychology, rooted in secularism, began to take over many pulpits, usually with a little Bible thrown in. Self-help books filled our Christian bookstores—everything from how to lose fat to how to overcome guilt. Some books were helpful, but the pursuit of personal happiness became an obsession. We formed a cult of self-worship in the Me generation.

The theorists Fromm, Rogers, Maslow and May helped us understand how to be self-actualized and maximize our own human potential. Many secular psychologists saw belief in God as a primary obstacle to reaching human potential. Sigmund Freud, considered by many a father of psychology, wrote, "If you wish to expel religion from our European civilization, you can only do it through another system of doctrines, and from the outset this would take over all the psychological characteristics of religion."[1]

Even God's character was redefined in secular terms. At first this was subtle, but eventually it was pervasive. God's love became God's tolerance. God's generosity became the heavenly bank account. Sins became mistakes, and demonic strongholds became problems. Anyone preaching on sin became a legalist practicing intolerance. To keep their congregations, some pastors softened their messages. To maintain interdenominational cooperation and unity, some evangelists lost their revivalist edge.

What does it mean to follow Jesus? He explained this critical truth several times to his disciples. Matthew 16:21 records, "From that time on Jesus began to explain to his disciples that he must go to Jerusalem and suffer many things at the hands of the elders, chief priests and teachers of the law, and that he must be killed and on the third day raised to life." Peter's response was startling. He rebuked Jesus. You would think by now the disciples would have understood the coming death and resurrection of Jesus, but they did not. For many of the same reasons you and I err in our thinking about God's purposes, they missed the foundational truths Jesus taught. At this stage, the disciples were still focused on temporal things, missing God's ways and eternal plans. They knew Jesus was going to set up his kingdom, but they thought it would be an immediate earthly kingdom. They expected Jesus to overthrow the Roman Empire, and then they would rule with Christ on earth.

Peter told Jesus, "Never, Lord! This shall never happen to you!" (v. 22). Jesus responded to Peter with a very direct and serious reprimand: "Get behind me, Satan! You are a stumbling block to me; you do not have in mind the things of God, but the things of men" (v. 23). Our problem is the same as Peter's. We do not have in mind the things of God. We think in temporal, momentary, self-serving terms and miss the depth and power of what it means to be followers of Jesus.

As he had many times before, Jesus explained to his disciples what it means to follow him: "If anyone would come after me, he must deny himself and take up his cross and follow me. For whoever wants to save his life will lose it, but whoever loses his life for me will find it" (Mt 16:24-25). In this one statement, he explained the enormous cost and the immense blessing of being his follower. He was not offering a benefits package to those following him, but a new life. To get this new life, we have to lose our old life. This is the incredible genius of God's plan. Unlike what he offered to

Moses and the children of Israel, which was only temporary covering for their sin, Jesus offers us a whole new life.

Christianity is an exchange of lives. I give up mine and I can have his. What an extraordinary idea! It is not asking Christ into my life, but Christ becoming my life. Do you see the difference? If I add Christ to my life by asking him in, I still have my old life and I'm still in charge. If I do what Christ said I should do—lose my life for him, lay down all my rights—then I can have his life. Let me say this another way. If I keep my life, I cannot have his, because true Christianity is an exchange of lives.

LIVING THE EXCHANGED LIFE

Paul understood the truth of living the exchanged life. He wrote in Galatians 2:20, "I have been crucified with Christ and I no longer live, but Christ lives in me. The life I live in the body, I live by faith in the Son of God, who loved me and gave himself for me." Paul understood that to have the life of Christ, he had to die to self. This is why Jesus, when explaining to his disciples what it means to be his follower, began by telling them that they must deny themselves. This teaching of Jesus is the opposite of what is often preached today. Many preachers only give the benefits while failing to explain the cost.

The nineteenth-century evangelist Charles Finney, though controversial, is considered by many to be one of the most successful evangelists in history. Why? Because more than 70 percent of those who came to Christ in his campaigns continued on with God. His two most common messages were "True and False Conversion" and "True and False Repentance." He explained in these messages that the person who does not change from self-ishness to benevolence has not been converted, because the God-given nature of the new life is different from the carnal nature of the old life. Finney also made a strong case that our conversion experience is proved by our personal piety. By the standard Finney used, many evangelical churchgoers today would not be considered Christians. Maybe he was right. Our Western definition of Christians has been reduced to everyone who believes in Jesus, regardless of how they live. And, believing in Jesus is often no more than ac-knowledging Christ's existence. It doesn't matter if they look like Christ or love him, as long as they say they are Christians or have prayed some kind of prayer somewhere. We argue that believing in Jesus in the biblical sense is placing one's complete trust in Christ as leader.

Jesus spoke of entering through the narrow gate: "But small is the gate and narrow the road that leads to life, and only a few find it" (Mt 7:14). This description gives no room for tolerance or selfish living.

Paul gave his definition of walking on the narrow road: "I want to know Christ and the power of his resurrection and the fellowship of sharing in his sufferings, becoming like him in his death, and so, somehow, to attain to the resurrection from the dead. Not that I have already obtained all this, or have already been made perfect, but I press on to take hold of that for which Christ Jesus took hold of me" (Phil 3:10-12). Sharing in Christ's sufferings is not a life of ease or pleasure, but a life of denying self. It is exchanging our life of sin and living in Christ's power. Pressing on does not mean lying back and enjoying all the benefits of the spiritual life without working out our purpose as believers.

Paul then goes on to explain how he participates in the exchanged life: "One thing I do: Forgetting what is behind and straining toward what is ahead, I press on toward the goal to win the prize for which God has called me heavenward in Christ Jesus" (vv. 13-14). This eliminates our inward pre-occupation and sets our focus on God's purposes.

The exchanged life is also one of obedience to God. John wrote, "We know that we have come to know him if we obey his commands. The man who says, 'I know him,' but does not do what he commands is a liar, and the truth is not in him" (1 Jn 2:3-4).

We must define knowing Christ the same way the Bible does. Who are we to change the criteria for what it means to be a Christian?

MODERN COMPROMISES

In coordinating or conducting nearly fifteen hundred citywide evangelistic campaigns, we have had the chance to survey evangelical churchgoers. Only about one person in twenty who claims to be an evangelical Christian shares his or her faith with others as a lifestyle. Many have never shared their faith a single time. Yet they are in good standing in their churches.

How is this possible? These people are living a life in disobedience to the commands of Jesus. They demonstrate with their self-centered lifestyle that they are not loving their lost neighbors, thus showing that they are not truly loving God. First John 4:20 says, "For anyone who does not love his brother, whom he has seen, cannot love God, whom he has not seen." Love is defined by laying down our lives for one another, just as Christ did for us. If anyone knows that his or her friends, coworkers and relatives are lost and on their way to hell but refuses to share with them truth that could change their eternal destiny, he or she may not be a Christian. That person is not walking in the love of God, because God's love is defined by sacrificially giving to others the greatest gift we have—the gospel of Christ.

What you're reading about the evangelistic gospel may seem too strict or even harsh, but it is mild compared to the messages preached for hundreds of years by those who came before us. I (Mark) have been a student of the teachings of Luther, Zwingli, Calvin, Knox, the Moravians, Wesley, Finney and many other reformers. They all used a much stricter standard for what it means to be a Christian. Over the years, their message has been compromised. Even as the number of people who claim to be Christians has risen in America, the moral standards continue to erode.

In Western Europe the situation is much worse. In Denmark, less than 2 percent of the population attends church. I recently had a conversation with a leader in the Danish state church. I was talking to him about the evangelistic campaigns we were bringing to Denmark when he asked, "Why do we need these campaigns? Everyone in Denmark is a Christian. They are members of the church." In his mind, simply fulfilling the sacrament of infant baptism and meeting the minimal requirements of church membership were enough to qualify someone as a heaven-bound Christian—in spite of the fact that few are living for God in Denmark.

These compromises exist in many cultures, including our own. In wealthy, white, suburban America, if someone is basically good and goes to church once in a while, he or she is considered a Christian. That person is even a better Christian if he or she tithes. In our African American communities, I have noticed a different set of standards. If someone supports the pastoral leadership—even if that leadership is wrong or even corrupt—he or she often qualifies as a good church member. So do those with money, particularly if they drive the right car or are musically gifted. I know these are stereotypes, but the truth is that the basic foundations of our Christian faith have been replaced by our nonbiblical worldviews. We value tolerance more than truth.

Now to be sure, no one who comes to Christ knows at that moment how deeply sin has infected his or her unredeemed life, or how completely Christ seeks to be Lord and leader. Much understanding and transformation occurs in the process of sanctification. But we contend that the initial decision for Christ, when made with the understanding that a transfer of allegiance from self to God is required, results in more sober, more complete and more lasting commitments.

PART 3

LET'S GO!
TAKING IT TO THE STREETS

7

PREACHING CHRIST

How do we preach Christ in this age? This chapter seeks to lay out essential elements for effective evangelistic proclamation in today's world.

The evangelistic message is first and foremost about God. There is perhaps no other subject we ministers address as important as the nature and person of God: Father, Son and Holy Spirit. We must present a true, balanced, biblical picture. People will make decisions affecting their eternity based on what we communicate regarding God's nature.

When we hear God mentioned by many modern preachers, it is usually in soft tones. He is portrayed as gentle and meek, which of course he is, but that's only one side of his character. Biblical truth has been changed to accommodate modern worldviews. To correct this, we must be sure of whom we preach.

The apostle Paul wrote, "Consider therefore the kindness and sternness of God: sternness to those who fell, but kindness to you, provided that you continue in his kindness. Otherwise, you also will be cut off" (Rom 11:22). The subject here is God's judgment of Israel in his acceptance of the Gentiles (us). This chapter in Romans contains a very serious warning and important insight into the character of God. It tells us Israel was cut off because of their transgression and indifference toward God. Paul compared Israel to natural branches on a tree that had to be cut off. Using this analogy, he warns us, "Do not be arrogant, but be afraid" (11:20). For if God did not spare the natural branches, he will not spare us either.

According to this portion of Scripture in Romans, God has two sides, both of which we must consider. One side is kindness and the other side is sternness. In our age, we are quite competently communicating the kindness and grace of God. However, we hear very little in modern preaching about the sternness of God. Maybe that is why there is so little fear of the Lord.

THE STERNNESS OF GOD

When Christ returns to the earth, he will not come as the gentle lamb, but rather will come full of the fury and wrath of God Almighty. Let's look at the description in Revelation 19:11-16, beginning, "I saw heaven standing open and there before me was a white horse, whose rider is called Faithful and True. With justice he judges and makes war." Here we have important insights into a different side of Christ, the God of justice who judges and makes war against those who oppose him.

The fact that this aspect of the character of Christ has almost disappeared in teaching and preaching has helped create our present view of what it means to be a Christian. We are rarely thought of anymore as "the army of God" but are only "the community of God." Too often Christian activity is only church dinners, camping and conferences.

Where is preaching about the ruling King with his measuring line of justice, having righteousness as a plumb line? Who talks anymore about the Jesus who, with a sharp sword that comes from his mouth, will strike down the nations—the One who rules with an iron scepter, leading his righteous army in battle? No wonder new churchgoers and Christians are so passive. The Christ presented to them is passive.

We are calling all Christian communicators to a rigorous reexamination of Christ. Follow him through the Gospels. Watch his actions; hear his words afresh. There you will witness both the kindness ("Come to me all you who are weary and burdened") and the sternness ("Woe to you . . .") of God. Let's preach a correct and balanced view of Christ. This is the first and most important act of public proclamation.

FOUNDATIONAL ELEMENTS OF THE GOSPEL

The term *gospel* is thrown around quite loosely in our time. Listening to many of the messages that are preached today, we could get the idea that any teaching that has a little Jesus in it qualifies as gospel. Other than maybe John 3:16, there does not seem to be any Scripture necessary in a message. Ministers can talk about the news, movies and their personal road to happiness without having to worry about quoting Scriptures. You would think we pick and choose the emphasis we like from the Bible. It seems that whatever is convenient or personally advantageous to the speaker or the listener is preferred. With these kinds of messages, preachers can fit comfortably in a secular world and their converts do not have to fear cultural rejection. What has happened to the biblical, traditional gospel? It has been lost and needs to be found.

We have identified five elements that should be included in a biblically balanced evangelistic message: (1) creation, (2) our rebellion, (3) God's love, (4) our price and (5) eternal judgment and reward. Presenting a complete gospel message will increase the chance of listeners experiencing a real conversion and walking closely with the Lord from the moment of their spiritual birth.

Creation. Presenting a clear, culturally relevant presentation on creation is the foundation of any decision for Christ. Today the theory of evolution has overshadowed the basic truth that God created us. If God did not create us, we are no more than animals, which means there is not a right or wrong and we have no accountability. There is no God who speaks and has a moral perspective. If there is no heavenly plan for humankind, we are merely part of a never-ending evolutionary process. Therefore people do not feel a need to change their lives.

Giving people the truth about human origins enables them to see the past, present and future as one coordinated plan of God. The book of Genesis defines our role on earth, gives God's parameters for relationships and provides foundations for scientific thought. Understanding life as created by God gives a new believer a comprehension of God's power and his control of the universe.

The biblical account of creation tells us who we are: "Then God said, 'Let us make man in our image, in our likeness'" (Gen 1:26). This means we are meant to have God's character and a moral view of life. We are destined by our Creator to be noble and good because *he* is.

Our rebellion. There is no way people can be saved if they do not know they are lost. Too often we talk only about God's love, forgiveness and benevolence, bypassing the less popular discussion of our rebellion against God. This creates all sorts of problems in the Western world. It confirms what people already believe: There is no absolute right and wrong—only different views.

Sin must be discussed candidly and openly. Right and wrong has to be explained by God's standards, with creation as the background. This is becoming increasingly difficult in a world that operates by relativism and situational ethics.

One of our campaigns in Sweden created a national stir because, while speaking, a team member read 1 Corinthians 6:9-10, which says, "Do you not know that the wicked will not inherit the kingdom of God? Do not be deceived: Neither the sexually immoral nor idolaters nor adulterers nor male prostitutes nor homosexual offenders nor thieves nor the greedy nor drunkards nor slanderers nor swindlers will inherit the kingdom of God."

Our evangelist did not single out homosexuality in this list, but that's the subject that made the press go crazy. Our organization received considerable slander, misrepresentation and outright persecution for mentioning specific areas that are evil in God's sight. The most discouraging part of this situation in Sweden was that some of the church community agreed with the press. The desire to be socially accepted often moves us to compromise.

We have seen pastors and evangelists try to keep people from feeling condemnation from their preaching. Yet, if someone is lost, that person needs to feel lost and condemned so he or she turns to the Savior. God gave Moses the Law, not so the Israelites would be saved, but so they would recognize their lost condition and turn to God. Paul wrote, "I would not have known what sin was except through the law. For I would not have known what coveting really was if the law had not said, 'Do not covet.' . . . For apart from law, sin is dead" (Rom 7:7-8). For people to know guilt and the corresponding godly sorrow that leads them to repentance, they must understand their own spiritual rebellion.

We should not present sin in a self-righteous or condemning way, holding ourselves up as the standard for holiness. This would be pharisaical. We should preach judgment with tears in our eyes, motivated by love. I (Mark) teach our evangelists to begin the discussion of sin with confession of their own rebellion, law breaking and failures. This lays a foundation of humility God can use. We have found that those listening to these messages relate most to the testimonies.

More than preaching a list of do's and don'ts, we are lifting up God's character, which is perfectly holy. This holiness is the standard by which all things are, and will be, judged and it allows the Holy Spirit to do his work. Jesus said, concerning the Holy Spirit, "When he comes, he will convict the world of guilt in regard to sin and righteousness and judgment: in regard to sin, because men do not believe in me; in regard to righteousness, because I am going to the Father, where you can see me no longer; and in regard to judgment, because the prince of this world now stands condemned" (Jn 16:8-11).

The exhortations found in 2 Timothy 4 seem to be written for our time:

> In the presence of God and of Christ Jesus, who will judge the living and the dead, and in view of his appearing and his kingdom, I give you this charge. Preach the Word; be prepared in season and out of season; correct, rebuke and encourage—with great patience and careful instruction. For the time will come when men will not put up with sound doctrine. Instead, to suit their own desires, they will gather around them a great number of teachers to say what their itching ears want to hear. They will turn their ears away from the truth and turn aside to myths. But you, keep your head in all situations, endure hardship, do the work of an evangelist, discharge all the duties of your ministry. (vv. 1-5)

Our ministry (YWAM) works with thousands of churches each year. Most of my weekends are spent speaking in churches in North America and other nations of the world. These churches represent a wide spectrum of denominations. While I (Mark) meet many great Christian leaders who are careful in keeping the integrity of God's Word, some seem to replace it with a one-sided, people-pleasing message. The attendees of these churches are often shocked when I discuss sin in specific terms.

As evangelists we cannot succumb to the increasing worldly influence in the church. Our message to the lost must include a clear description of sin in uncompromising terms. This is imperative if we are to see real and lasting conversions. A listener cannot know how good the good news is if he or she doesn't face the depth of the bad news. Now, for the good news.

God's love. The Bible tells us, "While we were still sinners, Christ died for us" (Rom 5:8). To a man or a woman drowning in sin, John 3:16 makes sense: "God so loved the world that he gave his one and only Son." To the hopeless, this is hope. To the guilty, this means the possibility of a pardon.

Last night I (Lon) sat in an auditorium listening to Billy Graham. After clearly diagnosing the problem of humankind—sin—he paused. Then for several minutes he spoke of the unconditional love of God in Christ. All around me I heard sighs of comfort as listeners realized the greatness of grace. Forgiveness of sins flooded the arena. The goodness of God overwhelmed us.

Convicted by the preaching on sin, many non-Christians in campaign audiences hang on to every word about promised forgiveness. The news about what God did in sending his Son, and about the price that Jesus paid on the cross, now has deep and real meaning to the listener. This is the part of the message where the speaker talks about the life Jesus lived on earth, his love for people, how he healed and delivered them mentally, physically and spiritually, and most important, what he did through his death and resurrection. These assure us of two things: Jesus is more powerful than death and the devil, and Christ is alive. In some situations, particularly in Hindu, Muslim or Buddhist nations, this is a good time to demonstrate God's power and love through signs and wonders. Recognizing the goodness of God helps lead people to repentance.

At this time in the presentation of the gospel, the speaker relates his or her own personal story of redemption. The evangelist holds in front of the audience the possibility of a new life and explains what God has done for him or her. This is usually the hardest part of the message for us to shorten. We can talk all day about the benefits of the new life in Christ, what it is like to walk and talk with Jesus every day, the euphoria of intimacy with God. This includes, but goes way beyond, temporal blessing or momentary happiness.

Our price. After preaching points 1, 2 and 3, the audience is ready for the fourth element, the price *we* pay. Because of current prevailing worldviews, this is perhaps the most important of the five. It must be covered thoroughly if the inquirer is going to make a deep, lasting decision for Christ.

We believe we need to stop separating the truth of salvation from that of lordship, because salvation requires a complete submission to Christ's lordship. Paul writes, "But what does it say? 'The word is near you; it is in your mouth and in your heart,' that is, the word of faith we are proclaiming: That if you confess with your mouth, 'Jesus is Lord,' and believe in your heart that God raised him from the dead, you will be saved" (Rom 10:8-9). Salvation and submission to Christ's lordship are one event. The Bible does not separate them, and neither should we.

Those to whom Paul was writing in the first century understood what lordship meant. If an individual or family gave themselves to a lord, they surrendered everything to him. Their rights, possessions, even their names were given up to come under another's lordship. They made this sacrifice willingly because they understood what they would get in return: membership in a new household with all its benefits, protection, security and honor. This is what happens when we give up everything to follow Christ. We are raised up to sit in heavenly places with him.

In YWAM campaigns, we train many evangelists, teaching them how to give an altar call. In their speaking they learn to use the same language

Jesus used and to preach self-denial through laying down their lives for him. During the campaigns, inquirers are told that everything must be surrendered to Jesus—their future, relationships, will and resources. Inquirers lay down all they know at the time; of course, more sacrifice and change will be required later as more revelation comes. This is not an easy gospel, but a powerful one. When people come to the altar, they should be coming broken, expecting a complete transformation.

You might think this kind of preaching would drive people away, but the opposite is true. We have noticed, especially among the younger generation, the harder this gospel is preached, the larger the response. Many young people are looking for something to live for, something worth dying for.

Eternal judgment and reward. This brings us to the final element of a complete gospel message: eternal judgment and reward. Until the inquirer, or even the Christian, has a good understanding of heaven and hell, his or her perspective on Christianity remains incomplete. Life can only be properly defined by understanding God's eternal purposes, particularly our eternal role. Ignorance of eternity causes two problems. First, if we don't understand heaven we have no hope. Second, if we don't understand hell we have no fear of the Lord.

The average Christian has little understanding of heaven and hell, leaving us with a temporal perspective, making us weak and easily manipulated by circumstances. Typically the beliefs of Christians on eternity come from movies or television, not from the Bible.

The biblical framework for eternity is not mystical and vague. Heaven and hell are literal places that are described in the Bible in significant detail. Old and New Testament writers went to great lengths to give us specific descriptions of these places, especially heaven.

Jesus' relationship with his Father was so close, and his fellowship with the Holy Spirit so intimate, that the activities of heaven seemed as real to him as those of earth. We know that Jesus' kingdom teaching referred to both the present world (the kingdom is near you) and the one yet to come (heaven).

Many of Jesus' parables are illustrations to help us understand this kingdom world. Jesus also clearly explained that everything we do here on earth affects our reward, and even our status, in eternity. Very few believers, much less unbelievers, understand this key kingdom concept. If they did, they would live differently. If we define the benefits of becoming a Christian only in temporal terms, we do an injustice to what Jesus taught, and we do not have much to offer unbelievers.

Temporal mindedness leaves us with complacent and apathetic church attendees, more concerned with sporting events and vacations than our God-given mission in this life. In contrast, Jesus and the apostles were continually focused on eternal destiny and the fact that they would be accountable to God for how they lived. As a result, they were sober-minded and willing to lay down their lives to reach a lost world. To them, suffering was not unusual, but to be expected. They considered it a small price to pay in comparison to their eternal reward.

This eternal perspective still exists in some parts of the world. For instance, the Chinese church teaches this worldview to new converts. This is one reason the church there is multiplying rapidly and looks much like the church in the book of Acts—devoted, filled with power and operating in the supernatural as they preach the Word boldly. All this in a Communist country that in many places forbids their very existence!

The story of the rich man and Lazarus gives us some insight into the realities of hell and heaven (see Lk 16:22-26). This story is an example of the way Jesus consistently described eternity. We can clearly see that paradise (Abraham's side) and hell were next to each other, separated by a chasm. One is a place of bliss, the other of torment.

Heaven. As proclamation evangelists, when we preach we don't have time go into great theological detail about heaven, but we should at least make our hearers aware of three things:

- The eternal physical condition: "He will wipe every tear from their eyes. There will be no more death or mourning or crying or pain, for the old order of things has passed away" (Rev 21:4).

- The eternal reward system: "Behold, I am coming soon! My reward is with me, and I will give to everyone according to what he has done" (Rev 22:12).

- The literalness of heaven as a place: "In my Father's house are many rooms; if it were not so, I would have told you. I am going there to prepare a place for you" (Jn 14:2).

I (Mark) add to my evangelistic message that everything we think, do or say has not only temporal but eternal ramifications (Mt 12:35, 37; Rom 14:12).

As followers of Christ, our future in eternity is awesome. Yet in more than a quarter-century of public evangelism, I have rarely heard an evangelist adequately present heaven to a lost audience. Why? We've heard some present-day Christian speakers say that people are more interested in this life than the next one. Therefore the explanation follows that we should focus our proclamation on "this life" benefits rather than on eternal ones. But aren't we responsible to tell the whole truth? Shouldn't our proclamation correct the error? Don't people need to know they are eternal beings? Paul thought so (see 1 Cor 15). By neglecting teaching on eternity, we are missing our greatest selling point of the gospel.

All of what Jesus, Paul and the rest of the apostles suffered makes sense only in the context of eternity. Paul wrote, "For our light and momentary troubles are achieving for us an eternal glory that far outweighs them all. So we fix our eyes not on what is seen, but on what is unseen. For what is seen is temporary, but what is unseen is eternal" (2 Cor 4:17-18). Christ's death purchased for us extraordinary mental, physical and spiritual benefits. Some of these benefits can be enjoyed now, but most will be realized in heaven.

Hell. The literal meaning of the words for hell—*Hades* (Greek) and *Sheol* (Hebrew)—is "the place of punishment." The teachings of Christian leaders and evangelists on the subject of hell have been just as inadequate as their teachings on heaven. This is very unfortunate, because television and movies present Satan and demons as mythological figures or heroes.

Rarely are they presented as the destructive evil forces they really are. In the minds of entertainment writers, hell isn't a real place; it's a fantasy.

Hell is very real. Revelation 20 tells us that eventually death and Hades will be thrown into the lake of fire, along with everyone whose name is not found written in the Book of Life. The lake of fire is the final hell. Many scholars believe it is the outer darkness Jesus spoke of, the place of weeping and gnashing of teeth. Scripture defines it as a place of torment and retribution. Jesus referred to it regularly, calling it a place of fire and separation from God. Paul adds that this eternal destruction includes total separation from God forever (see 2 Thess 1:7-10).

It is alarming that most people are on the road to this eternal destruction. Jesus said, "Enter through the narrow gate. For wide is the gate and broad is the road that leads to destruction, and many enter through it. But small is the gate and narrow the road that leads to life, and only a few find it" (Mt 7:13-14). This seems to be very different from what is widely preached in much of the world. (We speak more to this in chapter eleven, "Preservation.")

Jesus frequently warned his listeners about lifestyles that would send them to hell: living with unrepentant anger, unforgiveness, lust and hypocrisy, just to name a few. In the epistles, Paul gave us numerous warnings not to miss our inheritance in God's kingdom; for example, "For of this you can be sure: No immoral, impure or greedy person—such a man is an idolater—has any inheritance in the kingdom of Christ and of God" (Eph 5:5). Are the same warnings regularly given in messages preached today?

There is very little passion among those in the Western church for evangelism. One reason is because we no longer acknowledge or talk about the reality of hell. The idea that some of our loved ones, friends and most of the world are on the road to eternal torment, separated from God, should bother us. The great evangelists throughout history lived with the reality of eternity ever before them. It drove men like John Wesley and Dwight Moody to work tirelessly year after year "so none would perish." Let us ask the Lord to help us be mindful of the eternal, unseen world. The understanding of heaven and hell should shape everything we do. If it does not, we remain nearsighted and shallow.

THE INVITATION

The purpose of evangelistic proclamation is to persuade. Paul instructs us with this admonition: "Since, then, we know what it is to fear the Lord, we try to persuade men" (2 Cor 5:11). We want to persuade people to surrender their lives to Jesus Christ. We understand that the Spirit and other believers have been evangelizing the listeners for some time through their "prayer, care, share" witness. We now join them in the role of harvesters.

Because we are persuading, it is important early in the evangelism event to let the listeners know that you are asking them to consider Christ *today*. Often, before the message begins, the announcement that *today* or *tonight* you can enter into a new life with God is given by either the speaker or someone else on the team. We often tell the audience two or three times during the message that an invitation is coming at the end of the message.

Why be so redundant? There are a couple of reasons. First, it's not redundant to the listeners. They will hear thousands of words and view scores of images during the meeting. Telling listeners once at the end of the night that they can *now* respond too often results in information overload. They may not hear it, and if they do, they may not be ready to respond because it surprised them. Second, telling them often that an opportunity to respond is coming affirms their right to choose. It helps them prepare throughout the message. It also helps prevent us from being labeled with the M word: *manipulative*. No one wants to be tricked or emotionally forced into a decision for Christ. Therefore let us honor the listener and trust the Spirit of God, who is the one who calls listeners to Christ anyway. This is God's work; we are simply heralds.

There are many ways to invite people to the Christian life. Our method should be prayerfully chosen based on the size of the audience, the atmosphere and physical dimensions of the meeting place, and the accepted practices of the host organization. However, whether the response mechanism is filling out a card or coming forward, we urge that it be *public*. Quite honestly, if people are unwilling to go public at the hour of decision when the Spirit is calling and the mind, emotions and will are saying yes, chances are slim that they will go public after the event. Remember, we are not calling people to a secret society, but to a radical change in life that will go public within hours or days. When we are in Christ, and Christ is in us, it can't be hidden. This is probably why Jesus always called people publicly.

CONCLUSION

The five elements and the invitation outlined in this chapter are all important to a complete gospel message. The audience we are speaking to will determine how much emphasis we give to each element. For example, when I (Mark) am speaking to Hindus in India, I spend more time preaching on creation and God's love. Why? They already have a good understanding of evil and their lost condition. When speaking in Western Europe and America, I preach more on the subjects of sin and the price we must pay to follow Christ. Why? Because we are steeped in love of self, love of money and love of pleasure. Few people in the West see themselves as lost sinners.

We're not saying there is a strict way to present the five points. Different evangelists and organizations package these ideas in different ways. For instance, in appendix one you will find the Reverend Mr. Dallas Anderson's approach utilized in prisons. Young Life packages the concepts in their unique way for the audience they seek to reach. There are many other examples.

Remaining within biblical parameters, we can craft our message to most effectively reach our particular audience, but focusing on Christ and using all five elements with an appropriate invitation are, we believe, necessary at some point for a full comprehension of what it means to be a Christian. Let's restore the complete gospel message. When we do, we will see more deep and lasting conversions.

8

SEEKING RELEVANCE

The gospel of Christ never changes. However, the ways and means of delivering the gospel require continual adaptation. Different cultures, different generations, different eras (modern/postmodern) all require the evangelist to carefully consider how to deliver the gospel, both in local church and in itinerant settings. The late Helmut Thielicke reminds us, "The gospel must be preached afresh and told in new ways to every generation, since every generation has its own unique questions. The gospel must constantly be forwarded to a new address, because the recipient is repeatedly changing his place of residence."[1]

INEFFECTIVE PROCLAMATION

In some cases gospel preaching has become ineffective. There are reasons for this.

Bill (not his real name) was a good pastor. Serving in a struggling, diverse urban community, he loved his people and did a good job of reaching out to them. His church hosted several outreach ministries. They offered English classes, ran a food pantry, opened the church to an immigrant congregation from Haiti and offered a low-income daycare agency. I (Lon) thoroughly enjoyed my time in the parish and couldn't wait to worship with the church on Sunday. I found it hard to understand why the church was so small, barely viable in fact.

I had watched Bill love the people of his community. He was good at it and so was his church. But when he preached, something happened, and it was not good. His voice took on an unauthentic tone. He sounded like a nineteenth-century orator rather than the genuine servant I had been following around that week. The stained-glass tone was accentuated by his long, flowing black minister's gown, which seemed out of place in this neighborhood. He was far too regal for his marginalized congregants. There was no life in his preaching, little use of story and lots of fancy theological language. He reminded me of Emerson's preacher:

> A snow storm was falling around us. The snow storm was real, the preacher merely spectral, and the eye felt the sad contrast in looking at him, and then out of the window behind him into the beautiful meteors of the snow. . . . He had no word intimating that he had laughed or wept, was married or in love, had been commended, cheated, or chagrined. If he had ever lived and acted, we were none the wiser for it.[2]

HONESTY IS HARDLY EVER HEARD

Nearly 160 years ago Emerson understood what today's evangelists/communicators must get hold of. Listeners seek "real" speakers who talk conversationally. Oratory speaks *at* people. Effective communicators talk *with* people. Whether with a hundred or thousands, great communicators make each listener feel he or she is the only one in the room. My pastor friend's antiquated style separated him from his listeners.

Authenticity is the most compelling communication trait in today's world. The sincere evangelist who is nothing more or less than himself or herself flowing with God's power is the most effective. Evangelists and pastors seeking to preach to pre-Christian people have to get rid of any notions of "the preacher." Neither intellectual stuffiness nor finger-pointing tirades will work today.

A leading evangelism organization sent me a video of their "up-and-coming" evangelists. With high expectations, I watched the speakers. I was very disappointed because six out of seven used gestures and speech patterns from some bygone period of great Southern oration. They were all male and all white. They did not look like the America we now live in or the world we seek to reach, and they did not sound like anyone I listen to on the radio, watch on network television or talk with in the journey of my life. They were not being themselves. Thus they are marginalized and will not have a hearing in most of the world. It doesn't matter how good the message is if the messenger is perceived as insincere.

Relevance also has to do with homiletic design. Three interesting trends are developing in this area: the use of story, of more than one speaker and of the arts.

TELL ME A STORY

The first is the move from proposition-heavy preaching to storytelling. The Gospels are our clue in this matter. As John's gospel records, "Jesus did many other miraculous signs in the presence of his disciples, which are not recorded in this book. But these are written that you may believe that Jesus is the Christ, the Son of God, and that by believing you may have life in his name" (Jn 20:30-31).

It is the life and story of Jesus that contains the gospel. The original gospel stories were written for one primary purpose: that readers and listeners might believe in Christ as Messiah. Thus public proclamation that centers on the revealed stories of the life of Christ is timeless and powerful in its effect.

Narrative, or story, preaching is also the way Jesus himself communicated eternal truth. His use of parables fit well the content he delivered. Stories are a big enough container to include not just the facts but also the feelings and nuances of truth. Stories create immediate relevance with listeners. They employ the language of the day. They use the regular stuff of life and nature. It is my belief that narrative is the only container strong enough to carry gospel truth. Eugene Peterson speaks of the essence of story for communication:

The reason that story is so basic to us is that life itself has a narrative shape—a beginning and end, plot and characters, conflict and resolution. Life isn't an accumulation of abstractions such as love and truth, sin and salvation, atonement and holiness; life is the realization of details that all connect organically, personally, specifically: names and fingerprints, street numbers and local weather, lamb for supper and a flat tire in the rain. God reveals himself to us not in a metaphysical formulation or a cosmic fireworks display but in the kind of stories that we use to tell our children who they are and how to grow up as human beings; tell our friends who we are and what it's like to be human. . . . Somewhere along the way, most of us pick up bad habits of extracting from the Bible what we pretentiously call "spiritual principles," or "moral guidelines," or "theological truths," and then corseting ourselves in them in order to force a godly shape on our lives.[3]

Another value to using story as a primary component of preaching is that story crosses generations and cultures with relevance. For instance, a story about loneliness works with youth and adults, and works in Africa as well as Australia. Why? Because it deals with human need common to all people.

Proclaimers have always used stories in preaching. So what's the big deal? We are suggesting two things. First, the story of Jesus, which includes his life as well as the work of the cross and empty tomb, should be central in all evangelistic preaching. Second, story should not be used to support long, tedious ideas and musings, but should be the majority of the content from which the propositions or biblical ideas flow.

A CORD OF THREE STRANDS (OR FOUR)

The second development in the homiletics of public proclamation is the use of more than one speaker to present the message. In a world where attention spans are rapidly diminishing, it takes supremely gifted communicators to keep people listening for twenty to thirty minutes. As an alternative, some evangelistic organizations utilize two to five speakers to present the gospel. Each of the speakers takes one key point and presents it in three- to five-minute packages. This requires hard work from the preaching team but increases effectiveness when done well. It also provides the platform for persons of various cultures and races to join together to tell the story of Jesus—a story that is truly multicultural. When this happens, the church witnesses to listeners by the community it models in the preaching.

This homiletical design is used very effectively in at least two major evangelistic missions. YWAM's Impact World Tour includes primarily young believers in their twenties and thirties who are talented as skaters, bikers, dancers, singers and so on to bring elements of the message to the audience at different stages during a ninety-minute presentation. Often a more experienced evangelist will give the summary and invitation. Thus YWAM trains its performing artists to preach. Operation Starting Line (OSL) also uses this method. OSL is a coalition of more than fifteen agen- cies dedicated to presenting the gospel in every federal and state prison in America by 2010. The Reverend Mr. Dallas Anderson designed a five-stage presentation of the gospel and trains the platform artists—often musicians, humorists and ex-offenders—to tell portions of the gospel in "yard" events throughout America. Both organizations report superb response from lis- teners.

THE LOST WORLD IS A STAGE

The third homiletical design shift is utilizing several artistic forms to present the message, with the preaching itself considered an art form. Pastor-evangelists and itinerants have long known that music is a valuable means to deliver gospel truth. Today, where music, drama, dance, media and the visual arts can be added to proclamation, the results are often tre- mendous. For seekers, the other communication arts are quite honestly more attractive than classical preaching. It takes a lot of work to get people who are unfamiliar with, or prejudiced against, the art of preaching to come and hear gospel preaching. But the other art forms are the languages of culture. In such a design, preaching—or more appropriately, verbal communicating or sharing—is one of multiple forms used.

One hundred years ago Aimee Semple McPherson used dramatic sketches as part of her presentation. Willow Creek Community Church and other seeker-sensitive churches started using drama in the late 1970s and early 1980s. Dance is another highly visual and powerful means of communication. Again, Western culture embraces dance in all forms. It is time the church does the same. Whether it is hip-hop or modern, ballet or ballroom, dance can communicate in ways words cannot. With modern editing and projection technologies, it is also possible to use fine art along with the performing arts to communicate the message. Scenes from contemporary films do a better job of depicting the lostness of the world than can most communicators. In much of the world, especially the West, film has replaced fiction as the primary means of receiving and considering ideas. Many churches today are placing art exhibits in the lobbies of their churches as a sanctified means of presenting gospel truth.

Missiologist Donald Smith says that "all human communication occurs through the use of twelve signal systems": verbal, written, numeric, pictorial, artifactual, audio, kinetic, optical, tactile, spatial, temporal and olfactory. With careful use of multiple signals, the amount of information that can be presented increases dramatically. Perhaps even more important, the impact of the message is enhanced.[4]

I (Lon) often dream of developing a team comprising artists from the various disciplines who will, together in community, write and produce a series of gospel presentations employing the arts in the events. The goal would be to offer the presentations to communities desiring broad-scale evangelism events. Town, city, school or university theaters would be rented for the presentations. Preaching would be the primary art form, but in place of one twenty- to thirty-minute message, the evangelist would present the gospel episodically in the various "scenes" of the event.

The story would begin in the lives of real people facing real problems in this broken world. The next scene would transport viewers to the time of

Jesus, when he walked with people experiencing the same sorrows and confusions as we do today. The third scene would take the viewers deeper into their own lives—showing that, at the root of personal and global pain, sin spreads like an infectious disease in people and cultures. The next scene would depict the action Christ took on the cross to heal people and the world of sin. Then, a scene would depict what new life in Christ looks like—how old fears and polluted ways of thinking and behaving are replaced with good virtues because Christ who is alive can indwell every person who seeks his leadership in his or her life. Finally, the evangelist would give a clear gospel invitation. Each evening a new story or play would depict the same story. The opening scenes would focus on different felt needs, bridging to Christ as the only solution for humankind's felt needs (release from loneliness, poverty and so on) and unfelt needs (forgiveness of sins and reconciliation).

Imagine the potential impact on a city, as city-influencers who attend the theater regularly view their lives and the life of Christ intersecting on the stage. With God's anointing, many would be deeply converted.

TAKING IT TO THE STREETS

Formats for gospel proclamation are changing in today's world as well. Local churches desiring a steady diet of evangelistic speech should consider offering it outside the sanctuary. Many unchurched persons are miles away from accepting invitations to a local church, regardless of its architecture or accessibility. We believe that a person willing to attend a local church is already quite a ways along in his or her God-search. But when the church takes the gospel to the people, exciting things occur.

Affinity, or people-group, evangelism sees a community as a group of people who find commonality through career, culture, hobbies or special interests. Believers within communities become the impetus to hold meetings centered around their interest, where the gospel can be offered in a relevant and winsome way. Lots of churches do this to some degree, holding Christmas teas or MOPS (Mothers of Preschoolers) meetings, for instance.

Evangelists like Steve Russo and others who do this type of meeting take it a step further. They help a local church or several churches examine their congregations in the light of interest communities. Then these churches approach potential leaders of different interest groups to hold a meeting, usually around a meal to which believers in these communities invite their pre-Christian friends. The proclaimer works diligently to prepare a message that shows affinity with the group's interest, but bridges quickly to Christ, who is the "man for all seasons." The options are endless. A few groups that have been effectively reached include business people, tennis club members, parents of children with disabilities, golfers, triathletes and marathon runners, senior adults, parents of teens, couples, youth and children.

Whenever possible, meetings should be held outside the church building. Country clubs, banquet halls, living rooms, restaurants and pubs, bowling alleys, and health club lobbies are a few options. (For more information on this model, the Billy Graham Center offers explanation materials. E-mail bgcadm@wheaton.edu.)

Itinerant evangelists can also incorporate this model into their work. Notable evangelists such as Leighton Ford, Josh McDowell, J. John (from England) and Luis Palau have used this model to supplement their large-group meetings. I (Lon) have utilized this model extensively. The results are quite astonishing. Whereas large-group evangelistic gatherings may see up to 5 to 7 percent of those in attendance making spiritual decisions, at affinity meetings we see an average of 15 to 25 percent.

STAY TUNED

Another way local churches can enhance public proclamation is to utilize the episodic approach. While most perceive an evangelistic message to include a clear gospel presentation and invitation, many wise pastor-evangelists present the gospel over a series of weeks on Sunday mornings. The first Sunday presents a topic of great interest to people and especially pre-Christians (for example, "How to Have a Happy Marriage"). On the next two or three Sundays, the pastor gives helpful biblically based information on the topic, but always points to a relationship with Christ as the deepest answer to our need for intimacy. Each week the pastor-proclaimer invites listeners to return for the next installment—rather like a *Star Wars* or *Lord of the Rings* film series, each one building on the last. On the final week, the theme from beginning to end is the gospel of Christ. With the topic of marital bliss as the wrapping on the messages, the pastor reveals how our need for intimacy is ultimately a need for God. He or she also reveals that sin has caused alienation from God, but that God has done all that is required to repair the breach, if the listener is willing to turn from trusting in people and things and to submit all of his or her life to Christ. When a local church employs this pattern several times each year and prepares the congregation to invite pre-Christian friends, the joy of salvation surely will be observed.

PUBLIC PROCLAMATION "NEXT"

Itinerant evangelists can also learn from emerging models that appeal to contemporary believers and cultures that need Christ. In the mid-1990s, Billy Graham incorporated a special youth night into his campaigns. Under the leadership of Rick Marshall, a student of youth culture and former '60s radical, Saturday night with Graham took on a new shape. Titled "A Concert for the Next Generation," Saturday night's main attraction is now well-known bands.

The marketing deliberately casts Graham in a featured—but not headliner—role. This is because Marshall and Graham believe that in the last twenty years we have moved to needing the communicator-artist to support the communicator-preacher. Of course for Graham, as well as the artists, the only headliner is Jesus. The music carefully adds gospel content, preparing the youth to hear the proclaimer. The artists also give brief testimonies. The results are great. In nearly every Graham mission, Saturday-night attendance exceeds that of the other evenings. In May 2003 in San Diego, Saturday-night attendance was seventy-four thousand, while each of the three other evenings were about fifty thousand. Franklin Graham's festivals employ a similar Saturday-night focus, with like results.

Two other evangelistic organizations are developing models that appear to have viability today. The Luis Palau Evangelistic Association began doing BeachFests as the new century dawned. BeachFests combine lots of contemporary Christian music, as with Billy Graham Saturday nights, but add food and fun vendors, a skate park, special children's activities (such as face painting) and the compelling proclamation power of Palau in a festive atmosphere. These events are usually held over three days and last for several hours each day. Christians are encouraged to bring neighbors, friends, family and coworkers. Very creatively, the BeachFest model puts the gospel in three or four different places with different artist-evangelists proclaiming Christ, including a place especially designed for children and another for youth. Whether held in city parks or beachfront areas like Santa Cruz or Fort Lauderdale, these events attract a staggering number of attendees. This is not the only kind of campaign the organization does, but it is the newest and is gathering the most interest. The Palau organization now reports that its largest crowds are in North America.

The Palau organization has also taken the lead in forming an alliance for younger evangelists. These emerging evangelists share the resources of the Palau organization and often speak with him in large cities or statewide events. They also collaborate with each other in international settings. For instance, in 2003 a group traveled to India for two weeks of meetings in one of that nation's most needy cities. Palau didn't participate, but the alliance did.

YWAM's Impact World Tour (IWT) has designed a multiple-night model featuring a different presentation team each evening. Because IWT reaches primarily youth and young adults, the presentations correspond accordingly. One night includes Polynesian singers, dancers and actors who tell the story of Christ with amazing clarity. Their presentation of the death of Christ told through dance and movement focuses clearly and compellingly on Christ as Victor. The next evening, IWT uses a strongman team. The third night includes skaters, bikers and skateboarders, along with a hip-hop band and dancers. As shared earlier, four or five performers share a portion of the gospel message during each presentation. On some nights the different "acts" present together. The quality is very high, but these are not performances; they are presentations about Jesus Christ. It is not unusual for spiritual decisions to be made by 15 percent of the attendees. Impact World Tour sees similar results throughout the world. Because Western popular culture reaches nearly every community in the world through media, there are generally open doors for the gospel when presented through these forms.

SHOWING COMPASSION

Believers know that Christ and his kingdom are always relevant in every epoch and every culture. The world, however, must be persuaded. Today gospel speech will not stand on its own in convincing a lost world. It never has. Wesley or Moody, Graham or Booth—evangelists realize that demonstrating the gospel is crucial. Ministries of compassion, development and justice must go hand-in-hand with proclamation. Jesus proclaimed the good news and healed every disease and sickness. As Franklin Graham assumes more visibility as an evangelist, his message is authenticated because of his twenty-five years of compassion mission through Samaritan's Purse. It is hard to argue with a life focused on caring for the poor and needy. His mission of compassion opens the door for his proclamation. Today an evangelist needs to be part Billy Graham (proclamation), part Mother Teresa (compassion) and part Jimmy Carter (justice).

Evangelism leader Rick Richardson from InterVarsity Christian Fellowship developed a three-night approach to presenting Christ on campuses that utilizes compassion and proclamation effectively. The first two nights are targeted to present Christ to inquiring students and faculty through the arts, proclamation and personal testimonies. The messages are relevant and focus on dealing with felt needs. Christ is made clear. His work is explained. A call for response is given, usually by writing on cards, and many make solid faith decisions.

On the third night the tone changes markedly. Seeking people are invited to return and watch believers worship in song. This type of worship evangelism gives a great sense of God's presence. Seeking people are caught up in wonder as they see and experience the invisible God evidenced in his people. A time of preaching follows and again an invitation is given. But added to the invitation for salvation is a call to come forward for prayer for healing. Specially trained prayer counselors meet with, and pray for, every person who desires it. Broken bodies and souls saturate our world and our universities, and God answers the prayers of his people. This model is especially valuable in a postmodern setting, where the need to experience God precedes the need to understand him.

Of course, such prayer for healing is not new. Many evangelists, pastors and missionaries, especially in the Two-Thirds World, have always included such "demonstrations" of the truth in their campaigns. In the West, where skepticism reigns even in the church, it takes courage and rigorous honesty, especially when people aren't healed, to enter this arena of ministry.

Whether it is a local church wishing to reach their communities or an itinerant organization traveling throughout the land, every missional organization must offer the healing of both the soul and the body. The church is always strong when it does both. It weakens whenever it lays aside either part of the equation.

The healing power of God is as strong today as in the first century. We now devote a whole chapter to this sometimes controversial subject.

9

THE DEMONSTRATION OF TRUTH

What would the Bible be without signs and wonders? Can you imagine Moses trying to lead the children of Israel out of Egypt without the supernatural? There would be no plagues, no parting of the Red Sea, no provision of manna and no Ten Commandments. How effective would Joshua have been in leading Israel into the Promised Land without the walls of Jericho falling by the hand of God? How successful would Elijah have been without signs and wonders? Can you imagine him trying to confront Ahab and Jezebel without the supernatural drought?

What about in the New Testament? Think about how successful the ministries of Peter and Paul would have been without healing and miracles. In Joppa, Peter raised Tabitha from the dead, and the Word of God spread all over the region. Paul's ministry began with a supernatural conversion while on the road to Damascus. Signs and wonders accompanied Paul everywhere he went.

God's people have often been distinguished by the supernatural operating through their lives. This element is exceptionally important for evangelists, who minister to large numbers of people who don't know Christ. Unfortunately the Western church often ministers without signs and wonders accompanying the Word preached, thus ignoring a primary biblical pattern.

Some of our resistance in countries like America is due to our association of healing, signs and wonders with weird or dishonest people. We see someone preaching in a three-thousand-dollar suit, manipulating a crowd for personal gain. We have images of someone selling mustard seeds for one-hundred-dollar donations or sending scratch-and-sniff anointing oil by mail. Abuses like these grieve all of us, and they end up hurting Christ's image, but we can't let them overshadow our biblical mandate to operate in the Spirit's power.

CHRIST AND THE SUPERNATURAL

The book of Acts tells us, "God anointed Jesus of Nazareth with the Holy Spirit and power, and . . . [Jesus] went around doing good and healing all who were under the power of the devil" (10:38). Many would not have believed that Jesus was the Son of God without the supernatural element in his life. It was primary evidence that he was who he said he was. When questioned by John's disciples, Jesus pointed to his miracles as proof that he was the Son of God. Notice these words of Jesus: "Don't you believe that I am in the Father, and that the Father is in me? . . . At least believe on the evidence of the miracles themselves" (Jn 14:10-11). Then Jesus said something amazing: "Anyone who has faith in me will do what I have been doing. He will do even greater things than these, because I am going to the Father" (v. 12). This was clearly written to anyone who would follow him.

When Jesus sent out the twelve disciples, he instructed them to preach the kingdom of God and heal the sick (see Lk 9:2). When he sent out seventy-two others, he told them, along with other instructions, "Heal the sick who are there and tell them, 'The kingdom of God is near you'" (Lk 10:9). The pattern was clear: demonstration and proclamation of truth were to be combined.

Christ's disciples understood this and continued doing the works that he did. After being empowered by the Holy Spirit, Peter healed the crippled beggar. How did Peter heal him? He simply said, "In the name of Jesus Christ of Nazareth, walk" (Acts 3:6). He had been given the power of God to continue doing the works Jesus had done. The same is true for John, Paul, Barnabas and the rest of the apostles. Vital Christianity requires faith that results in operating in the supernatural. The early Christians understood that the advancement of God's kingdom happens by demonstration and proclamation of the truth.

ACTS OF COMPASSION AND JUSTICE

Demonstration of truth can come in many forms, including acts of compassion or justice as well as the supernatural. Unconditional love demonstrated in a variety of ways can have almost the same effect as a supernatural healing. More and more evangelists are following Billy and Franklin Graham's example of combining the preaching of the gospel with humanitarian projects. In fact, Franklin is known more for the work of compassion than for his proclamation. It gives him enormous credibility as an evangelist.

Another example of this comes from the spring 2003 Luis Palau Beach-Fest in Fort Lauderdale. Volunteers worked with Habitat for Humanity to build six homes before and during the proclamation event. Again, such work validates the gospel preached.

In my (Mark's) early evangelistic work in India, we combined praying for the sick with acts of mercy. To our evangelistic campaigns we added medical aid, well drilling and education. Parents were often overwhelmed with gratitude when they learned their children would be taken care of medically. Once their children had received vaccinations, they no longer had to fear polio and other diseases. New freshwater wells prevented the spread of many other illnesses. Witnessing these acts of unconditional love opened up villages and larger cities to the gospel message. Whole communities responded to the gospel as they watched Christians care for them in ways that their Hindu and Muslim neighbors never had. Showing compassion caused them to realize that being a follower of Christ made a person different.

ELIJAH'S DEMONSTRATION

Let's look at an Old Testament example of demonstration combined with proclamation. The Israelites had become followers of Baal and Asherah, pagan gods. Elijah had preached and prophesied to no avail; the people would not listen. So he took a different course of action. He prayed and it stopped raining in the land. After three years of drought, God got their attention. King Ahab had been trying to find Elijah to kill him, but now he had to find him so Elijah would pray and restore the rain.

Elijah told Ahab, "You have abandoned the LORD's commands and have followed the Baals. Now summon the people from all over Israel to meet me on Mount Carmel. And bring the four hundred and fifty prophets of Baal and the four hundred prophets of Asherah, who eat at Jezebel's table" (1 Kings 18:18-19). The prophet now commanded the attention of the whole nation. This set up one of the greatest power encounters in human history.

When the people had gathered, Elijah confronted them with their rebellion against God. But they didn't answer the charge. They were not yet ready to acknowledge their sin and turn to God. Then Elijah said,

> "I am the only one of the LORD's prophets left, but Baal has four hundred and fifty prophets. Get two bulls for us. Let them choose one for themselves, and let them cut it into pieces and put it on the wood but not set fire to it. I will prepare the other bull and put it on the wood but not set fire to it. Then you call on the name of your god, and I will call on the name of the LORD. The god who answers by fire—he is God." (vv. 22-24)

The people agreed to Elijah's test. He let the prophets of Baal go first because he knew how impotent their god was. For hours the prophets of Baal danced around the altar they had built to their god. They shouted and pleaded. The Bible tells the result: "There was no response; no one answered" (v. 29).

This is the moment when Elijah stepped up. It was time for the evening sacrifice, and God's prophet was ready. First the Lord's altar—in ruins from disuse—was repaired. Then a large trench was dug around the altar. Wood was set on it, and the butchered bull was laid over the wood. Everyone gathered around the altar to see what was going to happen. Then Elijah had them pour water on the offering, on the wood and even in the trench around the altar.

Elijah called out, and the Lord's fire fell. It consumed everything—the sacrifice, the wood, the altar, the stones and the soil. And there wasn't a drop of water left. Then the people, who wouldn't turn their hearts toward God by Elijah's preaching, fell prostrate at the demonstration of God's power. They cried out, "The LORD—he is God! The LORD—he is God!" (v. 39).

Has there ever been another case in human history when an entire nation was brought to repentance in a day? How did it happen? By bold, uncompromised preaching accompanied by dramatic signs and wonders. What a powerful combination!

MODERN DEMONSTRATION AND PROCLAMATION

My friend Dr. T. L. Osborn discovered the power of combining demonstration and proclamation when he began his ministry many years ago in India. Fresh out of Bible school at age twenty-one, T. L. arrived in the subcontinent ready to convert Hindus and Muslims. With his Bible in hand, he began to argue the case for Christ with these unreached peoples. As T. L. describes it, he would read from his black book and then they would read from theirs. Back and forth they would go, debating their beliefs. At the end of the day, no one's views had changed. This went on for an entire year; there was not one convert to Christianity.

Deciding that he didn't have what it took to be a missionary, T. L. returned home to America. Shortly thereafter, he and his wife, Daisy, attended an evangelistic campaign in America where the evangelist prayed for the sick each night. Many in the audience would come to the stage after prayer, testifying they were supernaturally healed by the power of God. This was followed by an altar call, where many who were lost would come to Christ. The evangelist would prove the reality of Christ and then ask for commitment from the non-Christians.

T. L. and Daisy realized that the demonstration of truth was the missing element in their missionary efforts. With new vision they recommitted themselves to the mission field, sold all their possessions and left America to evangelize the nations of the world.

The Osborns first traveled to Jamaica, where they conducted a large evangelistic campaign, but unlike before, they included praying for signs and wonders. The results were astonishing. So many attended the meetings that they could hardly handle the crowds. Many, if not most, who attended surrendered themselves to Christ. Hundreds of people were being delivered and healed by the power of God. T. L. and Daisy did not have to argue doctrine with the tribal animists; they simply proved Christ was real and alive.

As their ministry grew in the following years, they added large-scale mercy ministries to their work, supplying resources and humanitarian aid in their campaign cities. In doing so, they provided another example of demonstration pointing people to Jesus. They continued this pattern of ministry for more than half a century, reaching millions all over the world. Though Daisy has gone to be with the Lord, T. L. continues to evangelize today.

The Osborns are not well known in America, but the scope, size and effect of their evangelistic efforts are staggering. Attendance totals at their campaigns are some of the largest in church history. Consider this sampling of crowd sizes in campaigns: 130,000 in Holland; 200,000 in Nigeria; 90,000 in Japan; and 300,000 in India. All over the world, in more than seventy nations, for more than fifty years they shook cities and helped shape nations. They used the power of the Word with accompanying signs and wonders, demonstrating as well as proclaiming the gospel.

No one has officially added up the number of churches started as a result of their campaigns, but we personally know of nine thousand in just two of the nations in which they ministered. We're sure the total number is many times this. They sponsored more than 25,000 national preachers as full-time missionaries, who went out to reach their own tribes and villages.

Many preachers today pattern their ministry after the Osborns—men such as German evangelist Reinhart Bonnke, who recently reported that 1.2 million people gave their lives to Christ in a single day in his Lagos, Nigeria, campaign. By the local media's estimate, more than ten million people were in attendance.

Clearly people today are still very interested in the power of God when it's demonstrated. We believe that God intended his followers to be distinguished by the supernatural element in their lives. In a world full of philosophies, false religions and lies, truth must stand out from the others. How is this possible without proving what we're saying?

FOLLOWING THE BIBLICAL PATTERN

Much of the Western church today seems to be missing both the uncompromised preaching and the signs. Some church services, packaged in a one- or two-hour program, are void of the supernatural. Celebrating their departure from suits and ties to polo shirts and sweaters, churches have gotten caught up in focusing only on being more relevant to a secular world. God's presence isn't even necessary for their programs to work.

We are all for being relevant; much is written about the subject in this book. But while adapting to cultural change, we need to be careful to keep the power of the Spirit and the integrity of the gospel message. Paul wrote, "My message and my preaching were not with wise and persuasive words, but with a demonstration of the Spirit's power, so that your faith might not rest on men's wisdom, but on God's power" (1 Cor 2:4). If the decisions people make are only because of human wisdom or persuasive words, the result will not be converts who are passionate followers of God. According to Paul, passionate followers are produced when there is a demonstration of the Spirit's power accompanying the Word. All through the Bible, God's power is shown through signs and wonders performed by his followers. The pattern should be the same today.

GOD'S POWER DEMONSTRATED TODAY

The ability for us as God's people to operate in the supernatural is just as real today as it was in the first century. As Christians, we have available to us the same power Jesus used. Paul prayed for the church at Ephesus that they would know "his incomparably great power for us who believe. That power is like the working of his mighty strength, which he exerted in Christ when he raised him from the dead and seated him at his right hand in the heavenly realms" (Eph 1:19-20).

When I (Mark) was a young man, I read about healing, signs and wonders in evangelistic campaigns. They became very real to me later when I had a chance to operate in them as part of African and Asian outreaches in the 1970s and 1980s.

In the face of serious challenges, I conducted a series of campaigns in the Indian subcontinent in 1984 and 1986. We based our coordinating offices in the state of Andhra Pradesh. Our first outreaches began in Chirala, a small coastal community of 120,000 people that was ripe for the harvest. Almost half the population attended our three-night campaign, with more than twenty thousand committing to follow Christ. Many in the community were suffering from demon possession and were set free by preaching and prayer. The campaign in Ponnur was equally successful, though smaller and hampered by rain. The final community in our three-city tour was Guntur, which had a population of half a million people. We had scheduled an eight-day campaign, but it was abruptly interrupted on the third day by a national crisis. Our attendance had been building each day: first day, three thousand; second day, five thousand. At the rate we were going, we expected to finish with a crowd of almost thirty thousand by the final day. Hundreds of people were being healed and thousands more were coming to Christ.

This all came to a halt when Indira Gandhi, the prime minister of India, was assassinated. The city and the nation went into riots. We had to close the campaign early and flee the country for our own safety. Determined not to be stopped, we conducted another evangelistic campaign in the same region sixteen months later. This time it was in Vijawada, which had a population of more than one million. Vijawada is best known for its allegiance to the Hindu god Krishna. It is filled with Hindu temples and idols. This was the city visited by many Americans during the flower-child years of the 1960s and 1970s.

My nephew, Scott Norling, who spent most of his time living in India, served as my campaign coordinator. Scott secured a large field in the middle of the city for our eight-day campaign. He printed hundreds of thousands of handbills and posters and had them hung all over the city. He also rented a large sound system with dozens of speakers. They were mounted two stories in the air above the stage so people at the event and those in the streets beyond could hear the gospel message.

We began the campaign on a Sunday night. As I climbed on stage that night, I was accompanied by my wife, Karen, and Pastor Sam and Sheri Benson, who are our good friends. Sam, a powerful preacher, and I often took turns preaching during the campaign. This helped fill the three- to five-hour meetings that the Indian locals expected us to hold each night. They couldn't get enough of the teaching accompanied by signs and wonders.

With about three thousand people in attendance, the first night's crowd was modest by Indian standards. Sam and I preached from the Gospels, explaining who Christ was and what he did while he was on earth. We often illustrated the messages with drama. People loved the stories, especially the ones that included the supernatural. They were fascinated by the person of Christ, particularly the love he demonstrated to needy people by delivering and healing them. They were especially excited when we told them the story of Christ's crucifixion, his resurrection and that he is alive today in heaven.

We then began to prove that Christ is alive. I explained to the crowd that Jesus still ministers to people in the same way he did when he was on earth, by healing and delivering them. As followers of Christ, we could pray for them the same way he did because he lives in us by his Spirit. Next I prayed a prayer for healing over those in the crowd who were sick. I then asked for a show of hands of those who had been physically healed. To my amazement, hundreds of hands immediately shot up in the air. The next hour of the campaign was filled with praise to the Lord for what he had done. One person after another walked through the crowd to the stage to tell everyone how Jesus had healed them.

These supernatural demonstrations laid the perfect foundation for calling people to repentance and complete surrender to Christ. Almost every person in the first night's crowd of more than three thousand gave their lives to Jesus.

This powerful first night created a stir—both positive and negative—in the city. As you might imagine, those who were impacted by the power of God wanted more. They also wanted their friends and relatives to receive prayer. Everywhere our team went, we were stopped and asked to pray for someone. Sometimes we were mobbed by people with needs, much as Jesus was.

On the negative side, some of the civic leaders in the city who were Hindu were mad. They wanted the campaign closed down and us out of the city. They tried everything they could think of to accomplish this. They convinced the local police to pull our passports and attempted to have us deported. This didn't work because God had given us favor with a high official in the state who was a Christian.

On Monday, the second night, the crowd grew to almost six thousand people. As on the first night, we preached, prayed for the sick and called people to give their lives to Jesus. The response was the same—hundreds healed and thousands coming to Christ.

As incredibly exciting as all of this was, we had a sense in our hearts that God wanted to do more in the city. The next day our team spent several hours in prayer, asking the Lord to show himself in a powerful way. We all had a strong feeling that this third night of the campaign would be something very special.

The night began like the others, with people arriving two, even three hours early at the campaign grounds to find a spot close to the stage. The service was scheduled to begin at 7 p.m., but music began at 6 p.m. to help entertain the crowd. I usually arrived a little after 7 p.m. because the preaching began at about 8 p.m.

The car to bring me to the campaign grounds arrived. As I walked out of the front door of my guest home, I immediately noticed the dark rain clouds approaching the city. As far as I could see in every direction, heavy rain was falling like sheets from the sky. In minutes it would reach our campaign site. As quickly as I could, I jumped in the back seat of the car and asked my driver to get me to the grounds fast. He raced the two miles through the city, honking his horn the entire way. As we drove across the campaign field up to the stage, I noticed the crowd of ten thousand was starting to go home as the rain began to fall.

I prayed a short prayer: "Lord, what do you want me to do for you to reveal your power to the city?" Then I remembered what we had asked for in prayer earlier that day. Was this the opportunity?

I jumped out of the car with a new excitement. I found my translator, went to the stage and began to address the crowd. I shouted, "Stop! Don't leave! Let's pray!" Then with a newly found boldness, I prayed, "Father, I ask the rain to stop in Jesus' name."

Over the next few minutes the rain stopped, the clouds above the grounds parted, and we had clear skies. What made the miracle even more amazing was the fact that it rained in other parts of the city all evening but not at our campaign site. When the people saw this miracle, they pressed near the stage to hear what we had to say. All night long, God showed his power to those present. Sometimes the presence of God was so strong that demonized people would begin to scream or fall on the ground, like those we read about in the New Testament. Our prayer teams ministered to them until they were completely set free.

By the end of Tuesday night, we estimated that more than six thousand people had given themselves to Christ. Our prayers were being answered.

THE RESULTS OF THE MIRACLE

The next day the whole city was buzzing about the previous night's miracle. Interest in our campaign was growing. Wednesday night the crowd grew to about seventeen thousand. The meeting was once again filled with signs and wonders, as God confirmed the preaching of his Word.

From morning to late afternoon every day, Sam and I had been teaching church leaders from the region. Thursday afternoon, when I finished teaching, one of the pastors approached me. Grabbing my arm, he said, "Please come. Someone needs prayer." He pointed to a woman holding her three-year-old son. "She has waited all day with her son for prayer," the pastor explained. "She needs a miracle."

"What's wrong"? I asked.

"Her son was born without pupils in his eyes."

I wasn't ready for a need this large. I thought I might be praying for stomach problems or a headache, both of which are common in India. I was tired after speaking all day and didn't feel very faith-filled.

By this time, the two hundred pastors I had been teaching all day had come out and surrounded us to watch me pray. I took the toddler in my arms and prayed a short prayer, then returned him to his mother. Little did I know how God was going to take this brief encounter and use it for his glory.

The Thursday-night attendance grew again—to more than twenty-three thousand. Just like the nights before, many were healed and a large number of those who came to the campaign surrendered their lives to Christ. At about 1 a.m. I was finally able to return to my guest home and go to sleep. The next morning a loud pounding on the door abruptly awakened me. When I opened the door, I saw the smiling face of my Indian director, Chandra Bose. He excitedly asked me, "Have you heard?"

"Heard what?" I replied.

"Of the miracle."

I reminded my friend that we had seen many miracles that week and that he should be more specific. After he settled down, he explained to me that the young boy I had prayed for the day before at the pastor's seminar had received a miracle that gave him sight. Pupils had grown in his eyes!

The news of this miracle was spreading around the city. That evening an additional ten thousand people came, bringing attendance to around thirty-three thousand. The atmosphere at the campaign was electric. The woman went onstage holding her son, testifying about what Jesus had done. Some in the crowd were weeping; others were clapping in excitement about the miracle. They had a new understanding of God's love. Almost everyone in attendance wanted Jesus.

All of this so impacted the city that the next morning the Hindu civic leaders who had tried to close down our campaign came to ask me for special prayer. Kneeling at the entrance of my guest home, they humbled themselves before Jesus. Before the weekend was finished, we estimated more than ninety thousand people had made commitments for Christ. God had supernaturally touched thousands of these people. All of them had witnessed the power of God. I don't believe these results would have been possible apart from signs and wonders. The demonstration of the Spirit's power gave validity to the message.

SIGNS AND WONDERS IN HARD PLACES

Signs and wonders are especially important when we preach in hard places. My wife and I have watched the hardest Muslims soften when Jesus heals their sons or daughters. Nothing else has the same effect. In another Indian city, almost 100 percent Islamic, we witnessed more than twenty thousand come to Christ the same way.

The supernatural isn't just for poor, developing nations; it works in many different places. Recently African evangelists have been conducting campaigns in Western Europe. They often minister to the sick during their meetings. They are among the few evangelists who have had an impact in some of these post-Christian nations. In countries like Germany, Holland or Denmark, where the people are drowning in rationalism, there is a new openness to the supernatural. Recent reports from our campaign in northern Denmark confirm this. Our coordinator, Henrik Thomsen, tells of a thirteen-year-old boy whose leg was healed as a response to simple prayer. Even a national TV network ran a positive report on supernatural healing in churches. Healing is also happening in the United States, such as through InterVarsity's three-night campus events, described earlier.

This might be a good place to write about a major obstacle to operating in signs and wonders: lack of faith. Any missionary who travels internationally knows that healings and miracles are commonplace in parts of Asia, Africa and Latin America, while they're rare in Western nations. Why this geographical distinction? During his ministry years, Jesus healed many who came to him—in every city except Nazareth. Matthew 13:53-58 explains to us his limitations there. They did not accept him as the Christ, but only as the son of Mary and Joseph: "He did not do many miracles there because of their lack of faith" (v. 58).

It's been my observation that when a secular worldview takes root in a nation, city or institution, the working of God's supernatural power becomes less common. There's little or no dependence on an unseen God. These attitudes dominate Western culture. This gives very little room for faith and the supernatural.

KEEPING ON

Operating with Christ in the supernatural is not easy. I have tried and failed many times—maybe more times than I have succeeded. I would love to tell you that everyone I prayed for was healed, but that's simply not the case. But I can tell you that many were. There are different views on why this happens, but there's no one simple answer. I do know this: The problem is not with God's promises, which are always true, but in our application of his Word. I've decided what's most important is for me to continue to pray for the sick, deliver those who are bound, and believe in miracles as Jesus commanded.

Isn't everything in the Christian walk like this? For example, we have been given the fruit of the Spirit, but who is always loving, peace-filled or joyful? We don't toss out operating in love because it's hard. We know God commands us to love, so we keep working at it. It seems strange to me that so many in the church world are willing to throw out healing, signs or wonders when they don't always work the way people think they should. Do we just ignore the whole theme in Scripture, including all the commands given us to do the same works Jesus did? Can we claim we are Christians who live true to the Scriptures and still be satisfied without the supernatural operating in our lives? This would be hypocrisy.

Let's restore the complete biblical model God intended, with both the demonstration and the proclamation of truth. If we do, we will dramatically increase our effectiveness in evangelism.

10

SPIRITUAL WARFARE

M̲y (Mark's) views on spiritual warfare as it relates to evangelism were formed from two things: a diverse theological background and experiencing what really works. As a practitioner in evangelism, I've had to sort through many popular fads over the years that Christians call spiritual warfare. I've also had to respectfully examine many different theological positions on this subject. Working interdenominationally in public proclamation has exposed me to many different kinds of prayer and approaches to spiritual warfare. Often people with conflicting ideas are praying in the same room.

My background has allowed me to bump elbows with a variety of religious views. My grandfather was a Swedish Methodist church planter. I grew up in a Missouri Synod Lutheran home and was converted at my catechism graduation, praying a prayer that Martin Luther wrote. Several years later I went forward at a Billy Graham mission to make a public profession of my faith. In my teen years, I was affected by the Jesus Movement and experienced a spontaneous move of God. During those years, I was exposed to a gamut of supernatural experiences that helped sweep hundreds of thousands of young people into the kingdom of God. Later I was baptized in water at the Evangelical Free Church that my wife had attended while growing up. Add to this diversity my formal instruction under Christian Missionary Alliance professors and Southern Baptist Convention curriculums and my theological involvement with the Assembly of God denomination. Today I work with Youth With A Mission (YWAM), an interdenominational organization with staff in 170 countries, representing every imaginable Christian church background. YWAM itself embraces different aspects of spiritual warfare. I'd like to think this wide range of experiences left me with a balanced view. Of one thing I am certain: it did help me recognize views on the subject that lack biblical balance.

International work with YWAM has shown me that some Western or American views on spiritual warfare have come out of our secular framework. We are dominated by quick-fix strategies to spiritual warfare rather than substantive solutions that might cost us something. We've grown accustomed to drive-up-window Christianity, where we put in our order to "get it our way." Unfortunately we're exporting these ideas to other parts of the world.

This chapter is meant neither to be a full treatise on the broad subject of spiritual warfare nor to be an instruction manual on how to do spiritual warfare prayer. Many books have been written on that subject. This chapter is meant to present the case for public proclamation of truth as a crucial tool of spiritual warfare. We believe it is the most powerful weapon given to us, and it is often the most underused.

PUBLIC PROCLAMATION AS SPIRITUAL WARFARE

One of the great misconceptions about spiritual warfare is that it's what we do *before* we publicly proclaim Christ. We also think spiritual warfare is prayer, not preaching, when in fact it involves both. Spiritual warfare prayer is not an end in itself, replacing evangelism. We're busy doing prayer walking in our neighborhoods but failing to get to know our neighbors, expecting God to work while after praying we go home and hug the TV remote.

To understand how spiritual warfare actually works, let's examine the Scriptures. Jesus said, "If you hold to my teaching, you are really my disciples. Then you will know the truth, and the truth will set you free" (Jn 8:31-32). It's the truth we know that sets us free. Conversely, if we don't know the truth, we're not free; we remain bound, handcuffed by evil strongholds in our lives. Understanding why people are free or bound is at the heart of spiritual warfare.

Though we live in the world, we do not wage war as the world does. The weapons we fight with are not the weapons of the world. On the contrary, they have divine power to demolish strongholds. We demolish arguments and every pretension that sets itself up against the knowledge of God, and we take captive every thought to make it obedient to Christ. (2 Cor 10:3-5)

Strongholds exist in the areas of our pretensions, knowledge and thoughts. At their foundation, Satan's holds are lies. The first temptation in the Garden of Eden was the serpent lying to Eve, "Did God really say, 'You must not eat from any tree in the garden?'" Then he told her a second lie, "You will not surely die" (Gen 3:1, 4). Strongholds are *arguments* and *ideas* that are set up against the knowledge of God.

Another way to describe these areas is as worldviews. Worldview assumptions affect everything in our lives. If we believe a lie, we then live one. So how do we take these strongholds down? What brings down untruth? The answer, of course, is truth. The weapons of truth that Paul talks about in 2 Corinthians 10 are not of the world but have divine power to demolish strongholds. These weapons are truth proclaimed, truth prayed and truth lived. Jesus and his disciples did all three.

Truth proclaimed. There's only one offensive weapon listed in the Ephesians 6 description of the armor of God: the sword of the Spirit, which is the Word of God. The Word of God is truth. That truth is our sword.

The way we swing our sword is to speak truth (see Rev 19:15). When Jesus was tempted in the wilderness, three times he said, "It is written." When the world was created, it was formed by the spoken word, "Let there be light." And there was light. Before leaving the earth, Jesus told his disciples to "go into all the world and preach" (Mk 16:15). As important as prayer is (see Mk 9:28-29), Jesus didn't tell them to go into the entire world and *pray*. When Jesus sent out the twelve disciples, he told them to demonstrate and proclaim truth. He sent them out to preach the kingdom of God and to heal the sick (Lk 9:2). He said to heal the sick and to tell them that the kingdom of God is near (Lk 10:9). Remember that it was Jesus who said "You will know the truth and the truth will set you free" (Jn. 8:32). *Truth that you don't know can't set you free.*

Since Jesus' day, proclamation has been the most effective evangelistic weapon. As you read in the chapter four, the preaching of Whitefield, Wesley and others ushered in the First Great Awakening in Europe. These preachers were men of prayer, but the revival didn't come until they proclaimed.

All over the world, we've watched public proclamation change people, families, cities and even nations, particularly if it's accompanied by a demonstration of the Spirit's power through signs, wonders and acts of compassion. We've lost ground in the Western world because we stopped going public with truth. As we've said, we've kept truth within the four walls of our church buildings and have largely ignored the public arenas of education, the media and the arts.

The apostles were not stoned for praying; they were stoned for preaching. First-century riots were not caused by prayer meetings, but by the public proclamation of Christ and the corresponding demonstration of his power. We're tremendously encouraged by the increased focus we see on prayer. Prayer conferences and houses of prayer are emerging everywhere. Younger people in particular have a new zeal for prayer. But we can't stop there. We need to accompany it with going and proclaiming Christ to a lost world.

Most of us don't pray enough, particularly for the lost. Jesus sometimes prayed all night. The apostles had a lifestyle of praying every morning. And the Scriptures command us to pray without ceasing. The problem is that some have replaced the command of Jesus to "go and preach" with "prayer evangelism," somehow thinking this is enough. When we don't want to be troubled with the rejection, misunderstanding and persecution associated with proclamation, we ignore the most powerful weapon we have: public proclamation of truth. We must use both prayer and evangelism in their proper roles.

Light allows people to see. The enemy lives in darkness, and he wants the world to be blinded and to live under the dominion of lies. Ours is the kingdom of light. Jesus said we are "the light of the world. A city on a hill cannot be hidden. Neither do people light a lamp and put it under a bowl. Instead they put it on its stand, and it gives light to everyone in the house" (Mt 5:14-15). When your light shines before unbelievers, they "see your good deeds and praise your Father in heaven" (v. 16). Clearly light is supposed to be in the most public place, not hidden in a closet. But most of our warfare seems to be closet warfare.

Only when we proclaim truth publicly, accompanying this proclamation with prayer, does the light shine. For example, in the mid-1980s I was heavily involved in the pro-life movement in America. I was pastoring a church at the time and we, like many churches, would regularly ask God to stop the evil of abortion. I attended interchurch prayer meetings where people would often command the "spirit of abortion" to leave our city.

Then the Lord called us to go into the public arena and tell the truth about abortion—that it's murder. This is when all hell broke loose. Our church did sidewalk counseling in front of an abortion clinic, and the police showed up to arrest us. When interviewed by the media, I stated that abortion is taking the life of an unborn child. Because of this public stand, our church bus tires were slashed and windows were broken.

We need the same determination as the disciples. Remember Peter and John when they preached in Jerusalem? They were told by the Sanhedrin not to speak or teach in the name of Jesus. The disciples replied, "We cannot help speaking about what we have seen and heard" (Acts 4:20). Peter and John went back to the rest of the disciples and prayed Psalm 2. Then, Scripture says, they were filled with the Holy Spirit and spoke the Word of God boldly. It also says that "with great power the apostles continued to testify to the resurrection of the Lord Jesus" (Acts 4:33).

In the Gospels and the book of Acts, we see Jesus and the disciples publicly proclaiming and demonstrating truth along with their prayers, and the enemy trying to stop it. The instructions of Jesus to the seventy-two followers he sent out were to ask the Lord of the harvest to send workers into the harvest field. This means that even the prayer that accompanies our going should be focused on sending out more laborers. This contrasts sharply with the kinds of prayer often prayed by the church today. Much of our prayer is worded in such a way that we ask God to go for us or we command nations to be won without expecting to ever leave our homes or churches. We have become armchair prayer quarterbacks, telling the universe, and even God himself, what to do. But this is no more effective than shouting at a TV set to tell our favorite football team what to do.

Truth proclaimed and prayed. The mission that I belong to probably prays as much for nations as any Christian organization in the world. Much of this is done by the students attending Discipleship Training Schools (DTS), which are conducted in many different nations. When done in the school context, praying is always accompanied by going to these countries. YWAM's schools are designed so that outreach follows the lecture phase. This helps get people to the nations. YWAM authors, such as John Dawson and Dean Sherman, have written books that became classics on prayer and spiritual warfare. Their books are filled with stories of evangelism and missions adventures that demonstrate "praying as you go."

Paul prayed for Ephesus, but he also went to Ephesus at great personal sacrifice to proclaim the truth. His prayers focused on the people of Ephesus perceiving the truth that they heard. He prayed that the Ephesians would have a spirit of wisdom and revelation so they might know God, and he prayed for the eyes of their hearts to be enlightened (see Eph 1:18). A key form of spiritual warfare praying, therefore, is intercessory prayer for those who will hear the truth. Over the years, I have found this kind of prayer to be very powerful alongside the proclamation of the gospel. We know that "the god of this age has blinded the minds of unbelievers, so that they cannot see the light of the gospel of the glory of Christ, who is the image of God" (2 Cor 4:4). When these blinders come off, unbelievers can understand the gospel that is proclaimed.

Truth lived. When we demonstrate the truth of what we say, it greatly enhances our effectiveness. When people can see the gospel lived out before them, it opens their hearts to receive what we are preaching. That's why evangelism often depends on demonstrations of love. In campaigns in India, we noticed that many leaders in other religions ignored the physical felt needs of the people and demanded continual religious sacrifice. We responded with acts of mercy—helping with food and medicine, and drilling wells for clean water—along with our proclamation. Many of the people we ministered to noticed the contrast. In fact, even Hindu and Muslim civic leaders opened their hearts to Christianity because of public examples of Christ's love.

EXTRABIBLICAL SPIRITUAL WARFARE PRAYER

Most extrabiblical practices that might be called spiritual warfare are often done in the area of prayer. We have witnessed so many strange kinds of praying that we couldn't name them all. The most common would be in what some refer to as "binding and loosing." The Bible instructs us in Matthew 18:15-20 that we have power to bind and loose. But the passage is specifically talking about how we confront someone else's sin and what we do if he or she refuses to listen after we confront; it's not about warfare against evil spiritual forces. Scripture tells us, "Whatever you bind on earth will be bound in heaven, and whatever you loose on earth will be loosed in heaven" (Mt 18:18). We have the power to release a person from guilt or leave him or her bound. Jesus continues by saying, "If two of you on earth agree about anything you ask for, it will be done" (v. 19). This is clearly talking about church discipline of sin. (An example might be what's recorded in 1 Corinthians 5 when an immoral brother had to be judged.)

The misapplication of binding and loosing happens when we tie Matthew 18 with Ephesians 6:12, which tells us our "struggle is not against flesh and blood, but against the rulers, against the authorities, against the powers of this dark world and against the spiritual forces of evil in the heavenly realms." When these two Scriptures are taken out of context and put together, we often conclude that we're supposed to bind and loose the principalities of darkness in the heavenly realms. But, of course, this isn't what Scripture teaches.

Many things can affect these unseen principalities. George Otis Jr., in his study of moves of God around the world, has defined consistent patterns when transformations are seen in communities. He points out that the spiritual climate of a city can be affected by group prayer (see Acts 4:23-31), acts of unconditional love, even martyrdom. In his writings, Dawson points out the importance of reconciliation toward offended peoples and the necessity of breaking unholy covenants that may have been established by previous generations.

I've often wondered why so many people believe we can simply command a principality over a region to leave and it will, when Scripture gives no example of that. If we could really command the principalities over cities and nations, we would have certainly seen Jesus and the apostles do it. But they never did. In fact, there is no example of it in the entire Bible. We do get a glimpse of the heavenly realm when Daniel prayed and God sent Michael, the warring angel, to answer his prayer. The prince of the Persian kingdom, a high member of Satan's realm, resisted Michael. Nowhere does the passage say that Daniel or his prayers had any authority over that prince. We see throughout Scripture that our prayer, praise, thanksgiving and intercession do move God. We also see that our prayer affects the kingdom of darkness. But the power to command unseen principalities rests with the Lord.

We have many examples of times when Jesus and the disciples ministered personal deliverance and commanded demons to leave. These acts were done on a one-to-one ministry level. Why can't we do the same on a corporate level? The strongholds of hell over regions or nations involve many human choices. As an example, holds of lust that dominate the Western world are the result of people deciding to live lustful lives. If we could bind a spirit of lust over a region (and we cannot), the binding would last only a second as thousands of people made more lustful choices. Greed dominates much of the world, leaving many in poverty. Our nations will only be free from its hold when people become benevolent. How will this happen? By commanding a spirit of greed to leave? No. It happens when people hear and see the truth and choose to respond to it. The reason the proclamation of truth is such a powerful spiritual weapon is because when a family, city or nation hears the truth and obeys it, the holds of hell lose their grip. Worldviews change to God's perspective, so evil forces have no right or ability to hold people anymore. The truth proclaimed, understood and responded to in any area is the key to freedom. Jesus made this clear when he told us we will know the truth and the truth will set us free.

In the book of Revelation is one of the clearest statements about what overcomes Satan. The apostle John explained to us that the accuser of the brethren was brought down by these things: "They overcame him by the blood of the Lamb and by the word of their testimony; they did not love their lives so much as to shrink from death" (Rev 12:11). Listed first is what Jesus did: the shedding of his blood. Second and third are what the disciples (and you and I) do: testify (proclaim) and lay down our lives. The enemy can't stand up against these three things.

The spiritual warfare we see in Scripture and the kind that works in our day are the same. If we reach out to the world the way the apostles did, we'll have the same results. Mark 16:20 tells us, "The disciples went out and preached everywhere, and the Lord worked with them and confirmed his Word by the signs that accompanied it." They upended their world. Fervent prayer, public proclamation and demonstrations of truth together really work; they change the world.

11

PRESERVATION

This book addresses the complex responsibility of gospel proclamation—a task so difficult only Christ can accomplish it through us. But the proclamation of the gospel is not the end of the process. Another difficult task remains: the evangelist or the preacher who proclaims must help facilitate the ways and means to mature and preserve the faith of persons making decisions for Christ.

NOBLE ATTEMPTS TO PRESERVE THE HARVEST

As we've noted earlier, the Billy Graham Evangelistic Association teaches that 45 percent of the effort in a campaign is preparation, 10 percent is proclamation, and a full 45 percent is follow-up, or preservation. Nearly half of the effort needs to focus on preserving the harvest. Anyone associated with a Graham campaign knows how extensive, immediate and urgent the follow-up is to the leadership. I (Lon) have watched and analyzed the process, and it is very impressive. (In appendix two we've included a more detailed report of the many phases in this process.) Gary Cobb, who directs the counseling and follow-up for Graham festivals, is relentless in his desire to see every person who makes a faith decision become incorporated into a local church. Other major campaign organizations have the same values. They are passionate about it.

SAD REALITIES

Yet with all the effort expended, it is quite discouraging to see that a number of inquirers apparently never join a Christian community where the faith is taught and modeled for them. My coauthor Mark Anderson of YWAM's Impact World Tour assesses that, on average, about a third of those making faith decisions at public meetings are very serious regarding Christ. Another third are somewhat serious, though less sure about what is happening, both on the emotional and cognitive levels. The last third go forward, but more from emotion or because a friend urges them than because a true volitional decision has transpired.

Cobb concurs with Anderson, though both are quick to add that this is more their perception than any sort of fact proven by quantitative analysis. As discussed in chapter five, close studies of the 1976 Graham campaign in Seattle that were conducted by a sociologist on behalf of the organization revealed that 18 percent of those recording decisions actually joined a local congregation. Less than 20 percent! While several factors and variables must be understood, the results are discouraging and even heartbreaking. Remember that these results came from the labors of arguably the most efficient evangelistic organization in the world. Since then the organization has added other measures to increase the retention percentage. The goal is to see 100 percent of those who make decisions join a local faith community.

UNIVERSAL MALADY

The preservation problem holds as true for local churches as it does for evangelistic organizations. As former pastors, we have seen firsthand the disconnect between faith decisions and faith practice. We've called, knocked on doors, and given church welcoming gifts of books, coffee mugs and homemade cookies to display Christian love and hospitality to inquirers. Sometimes our efforts resulted in new believers returning to churches of their past or other faith communities in our cities. That is great, because there is really only one church in any community; it just meets in many locations. But far too often, the inquirers simply drop out of sight, the early glow of a spiritual decision fades, and they return to life apart from God. One denominational leader lamented that in 1993 his denomination recorded more than three hundred thousand faith decisions. But a year later, they couldn't locate more than three thousand (1 percent) of these inquirers in their churches. Proclamation evangelists and church pastors have been debating and lamenting these realities for years.

Books such as *What's Gone Wrong with the Harvest?* by James Engel and Wilbert Norton address these issues. They raise many questions, such as what does belief look like? Some streams of the church argue that participation in the sacrament of baptism is the outward sign of inner regeneration. The sign of outer works then substantiates or supports the baptism. Others, especially evangelicals, argue that saving faith occurs as one "receives Christ" or "trusts Christ." They would say there are many ways one expresses the desire to know Christ. This invisible "faithing" is validated with the outward sign of "praying the prayer," "coming forward," "raising a hand," "signing a card" and so on.

We don't believe that either a sacrament apart from faith or praying a prayer without faith is sufficient. In many ways, the whole church has fallen into "easy believism." Actually no one can unmistakably verify saving faith, because it is the invisible work of God within the inquirer. Yet the Scriptures suggest many marks of belief. It's important to note that none of these marks are necessarily identifiable at the moment of decision. They will occur if regeneration occurred, but the timing of their appearance differs. It is therefore even more important for the inquirers to be linked with God's people as soon as possible after the faith decision. Care-driven follow-up is one way to assure that a faith decision is, or becomes, saving faith.

Rick Richardson, national evangelist for InterVarsity Christian Fellowship, others and I are doing important thinking on this topic. We suggest at least four marks of saving faith or initiation into Christ's kingdom:

1. *Union with Christ.* A person in Christ is aware of a relationship with God that is different than before his or her commitment. It is personal and in some way approximates intimacy with God. For some believers raised in healthy Christian climates, there is no time they did not

sense this closeness. For such people, saving faith occurred early in their lives (see Jn 14:20).

2. *Conviction, forgiveness and gratitude.* Saving faith results in abiding humility. The believer is aware of how deep and continual God's forgiveness is. Conviction of sin evident at initiation only grows after conversion. Godly sorrow follows, and gratitude and praise for God's kindness never cease (see 1 Cor 15:8-10).

3. *Leadership of Christ.* The new life is evidenced by a life that looks new. Again, it takes a lifetime and then some to grow into Christlikeness, yet the Bible argues that almost immediately one's life takes a turn for the better. We are no longer controlled by a sin nature. The new believer starts loving God, and Christ dwells in him or her; therefore obedience to God's ways begins to show itself (see Rom 6:11-14; 1 Jn 2:3-6).

4. *Commitment to community.* The new believer hungers for God, and also starts to desire community or fellowship with God's people. Baptism is baptism into Christ's body, the church. This, too, is a mark of belief. Just as we love our family and desire to be with them, the convert starts desiring life with the new and eternal family (see 1 Cor 12:13; 1 Jn 1:3-4).

Besides questions of what belief looks like, other questions arise. Is proclamation evangelism too impersonal to provide adequate nurture for inquirers? Maybe the problem of inquirer drop-off is not the failure of public evangelism ministries but of local churches leading the preservation teams, who don't follow up on those who made decisions. Or is the problem that the majority of churches who do follow up on new believers don't know quite how to incorporate them into the fabric of church life? Perhaps some people in the local church are desiring to incorporate new believers, but the systems and the structures of the church unconsciously put up barbed wire? Who is to blame and how do we fix it? Can it be fixed?

As stated earlier, the truth is that no one division of the church seems to do a very good job of moving seekers to become fully devoted believers. Blame belongs everywhere. So before we cast too many stones, perhaps we should examine some biblical content on this issue. Isn't this what Jesus was discussing when he gave us the parable of the sower? We are utilizing the Synoptics for this analysis, drawing parallels and unique contributions from the three texts (Mt 13:1-23; Mk 4:1-20; Lk 8:4-15).

FIRST-SOIL EROSION

When the seed is sown in the first soil, it is quickly snatched away by Satan. The quickness of this attack is alarming. The listener seems to have little time to respond. The problem is that the listener doesn't understand the gospel (Mt 13:19). Whose fault is this? Surely this is an admonition to evangelists/preachers. We must work hard to make the gospel clear and relevant to the listener. Paul was so concerned about this, he asked for prayer that he would proclaim clearly (see Col 4:4).

But Jesus tells us this failure is primarily the doing of Satan. In all three passages, the evil one comes and snatches away the word: "The thief comes only to steal and kill and destroy" (Jn 10:10). We should not expect the enemy to sit passively by as we attempt to pull people from hell to heaven. In fact, he "has blinded the minds of unbelievers, so that they cannot see," they cannot understand (2 Cor 4:4). This is a cosmic issue, and the evil one laughs as evangelists blame local churches, while churches and parachurch organizations blame evangelists for the lack of preservation. The truth is, there is another player in the field. When we are sharing the gospel with a person who seems genuinely interested but unable to understand, we should be aware that the evil one is active.

Usually we would describe first-soil people as those who don't respond or make decisions of any kind. When the speaker invites people forward, these listeners head for the door. Or they raise a hand or come forward at a meeting, but there's no interest in further talk and no movement toward the things of God. Yet the Luke passage, especially, suggests that the Word finds some residence in the heart, for "the devil comes and takes away the word from their hearts" (Lk 8:12). There must be some degree of acceptance or at least interest in the message, but it is short-lived.

How do we fight against the devil's attacks on people who are seeking? As mentioned above, we must be clear and relevant in our communication. This is not easy, as the evangelistic address is very complex. Perhaps that's why Paul calls it a mystery (see Col 4:3-4). But more importantly, this is a call to warfare prayer. The saints must intercede before, during and after gospel proclamation to thwart the enemy's desire to snatch away the seed of the gospel. Never is spiritual warfare more real than when the gospel is being proclaimed. Every communicator of Christ must give great attention to organizing intensive and broad-scale prayer for the proclamation event.

A pastor once told me he believed the first forty days after a commitment to Christ are the most dangerous, and that the evil one works harder in that period, seeking to snatch away the Word sown in the heart. I confess not liking the reality of the first soil. I'd rather believe that the characters in the salvation act are limited to God and lost people. But Jesus won't allow such a limited view. C. S. Lewis said it best: "There is no neutral ground in the universe: every square inch, every split second, is claimed by God and counterclaimed by Satan."[1] No, a third actor is present in the struggle for souls, and he is a frightening and effective foe.

SECOND-SOIL EROSION

Many readers know stories of people who respond to the gospel by walking forward at a meeting or raising their hand at an invitation. They pray the prayer. It seems genuine, with at least some enthusiasm or wonder at what happened. But nothing happens after that. They don't show up at church or come back to the Alpha Course meeting. They don't read the materials or Scriptures given to them. They don't return the calls of loving saints who wish to walk with them in the early stages of Christian life. There is no life. The blindness remains.

Last year my wife and I (Lon) had the occasion to walk a couple toward

Christ. Initially the man seemed more interested than the woman. He asked good questions and immediately brought his girlfriend and their family to church. It looked like the beginning of a good salvation story. But early openness quickly closed. He seemed to harden against the message as quickly as he'd shown openness. I don't know how to explain it. Even as I write, I pray for his salvation. But now I see only hard ground, where once was soft soil.

I can't blame his hardness on the church. We loved deeply and spent lots of time nurturing the seed. Early enthusiasm turns hard, cold and dead. The story is the same for the man's girlfriend. She "wanted" to become a Christian. My wife shared the gospel with her and prayed with her to receive Jesus. We had the family into our home and sought opportunity to assist them in their spiritual lives as well as in areas of life where they had problems. But now, only a few months later, there is no sign of them. The only communication occurs when we initiate it, and even then it is merely peripheral.

Jesus speaks of such persons as second-soil people. Second-soil people show all the early signs of regeneration, especially joy. But all too quickly, they close up. In the sower parable, Jesus states that tribulation and persecution are the causes of the collapse (Mt 13:21; Mk 4:17). Luke 8:13 calls it temptation or a time of testing. But the problems are because of "the Word." Something about the Christian message, something in its implications impacts the lives of the responders, and they choose to turn away. In areas of the world where overt persecution against Christians exists, this falling away is explainable, though regrettable. If one's new faith results in loss of relationships with family, in loss of career or in threats on one's life, then we can understand the struggle. Jesus said he came to bring a sword and not peace; family systems will at times be torn apart (see Mt 10:34-37). Rugged persecution causes many to fall away.

But in religiously free societies, this quick falling away also occurs, though the reasons are less apparent. According to Jesus, it is still because of the Word. The Word is sharper than a double-edged sword, cutting deeply into souls (see Heb 4:13). The Word judges us and we must respond rightly. Many new responders to the message of Christ desire the consolations of faith but not the requirements. Because they do not immediately grow in the knowledge of faith, thereby understanding that even the requirements of the faith are actually beneficial for life and made possible by the indwelling Spirit, they are in danger of falling away.

In the case of the couple I described, the writing was on the wall. The early enthusiasm for Christian faith ebbed quickly because of the implications of the Word. First, they were living together outside of marriage with one of them bringing three children to the equation. Second, they were from very different cultural backgrounds in which expectations about marriage and parenting were poles apart. This impacted not only their relationship but also the woman's children and their relationship to the man. Finally, important choices for the family's welfare needed to be made. The Word was clear on priorities. The couple chose differently. The results were tragic for the relationship and the children.

The verdict is still out. Was the woman saved? There are no signs she was, except that she willingly prayed a prayer to receive Christ. Regardless of evangelical formulations, we know that a decision or prayer does not make a commitment. No fruit is apparent. The man didn't get as far as the woman, never making a decision for Christ, at least as far as we know. God can still redeem them and save this family. We won't give up in our prayers or other efforts. But sadly, the two appear to be second-soil casualties.

It is interesting that Jesus places the blame for second-soil people directly on them. Satan receives no credit for the collapse, nor is the community of faith the culprit. The seeking people come up against the good requirements of the faith and, tragically, turn away.

THIRD-SOIL EROSION

Third-soil people hear the Word too. But, like second-soil people, they do not mature. In fact, something happens that makes the Word seem unfruitful. In reality, the problem is not the Word, but other competing habits and loves that choke out the good news of the reign of Christ. All three Gospel texts state that worry is a major culprit. For a time, when the freshness of spiritual faith is intoxicating, some people may be drawn to the Christian life. But if such people do not learn how to "rest in the Lord" concerning the cares of life, they will fall away. Worry, anger or playing the victim in a hard world replaces Christian hope. Christians are not exempt from the struggles of life, but they learn to give their worries to the Lord of the universe and rest in him, knowing he is in charge and will save them. Sadly, people raised to be independent and self-made don't easily come to the point of absolute surrender. Until they do, worry dominates their souls. Soon God is rejected as impotent.

The texts also state that delighting in riches and pleasures will choke out the Word. I've heard it said that Christians in the West are third-soil people because of our addiction to pleasure and wealth. For such people, an initial attraction to Christ is primarily because he is a delight and pleasure. There is a wonder that comes with believing in Christ. But the danger here is that this delight simply feeds an addiction. Such responders to the message desire Christ as *another* pleasure, *another* add-on to already pleasure-saturated lives. Soon, however, the demands of the Word confront the addiction, and the responders must choose. Jesus will not leave us in our hedonism; he calls responders to lives of sacrifice. The Christian worldview soon confronts Western materialism. Christ is never an add-on, never just another pleasure. He must become the center of life, and he resists all attempts to make him one of the gang.

Jim and Terri (not their real names) took clear, definitive steps toward Christ. Jim especially showed the fruits of faith with his love for the Scriptures and fellowship. These loving parents brought their children to Sunday school and church faithfully. They served in the church. Still, after a period of time, something was amiss. They loved new cars, expensive vacations, lots of parties with too much alcohol and all the trappings of wealth. Jim was a faithful attendee in a small group, but it became clear his love for the Word was waning. He liked the fellowship, but began to struggle against the Word. The truth was lovingly taught them, but disobedience to the Word became commonplace. The pursuit of pleasure led toward alcohol abuse. The desire for things made them less-than-generous givers of their resources. Marital problems surfaced, but instead of dealing with them, the couple kept on existing and repressed growing resentments. Today they are divorced. Both are in adulterous relationships. Their precious children bear the scars of parents lost in third-soil sin. As Jesus sadly points out, they have not matured (see Lk 8:14).

Still our prayers attend them. The Word and a loving but honest church are confronting them. The verdict is out. It could go either way. Repentance is a miraculous healer, but time is short.

Once again, Jesus places the problem of preservation squarely on the shoulders of the individuals who make the faith decisions. He does this because the resources of God, including the Holy Spirit, the angels, the Word and the church with its many graces, are more than sufficient to "keep you from falling" (Jude 24).

FOURTH-SOIL PRODUCTION

Thankfully the story does not end without hope. There is a fourth soil. Those fitting this metaphor "hear the word, retain it, and by persevering produce a crop" (Lk 8:15). Matthew (13:23) and Mark (4:20) add that these fourth-soil saints become reproducers who bring in crops thirty-, sixty- or a hundred-fold. Every evangelist and pastor proclaiming Christ longs to see fourth-soil saints. We long for them so much that we experience great guilt when we don't see this kind of soil more often. I fear that, in our longing, we put the full responsibility for failure on the church and its resources, or lack thereof. While it is vital that we create and sustain superior preservation resources, we do well to see the problem of preservation in a more comprehensive way. The parable of the sower makes it clear that both Satan and especially the seeker (or responder) play significant roles in spiritual erosion.

Of the four soils in the story, only one produces a crop. It appears that only fourth-soil people are true disciples. We can't press this story too far by declaring that only one of four who make a faith decision will become a fully committed Christ follower. Nevertheless Jesus told this story emphasizing that more fall away than follow. Other passages support this sad reality. Jesus said, "Enter through the narrow gate. For wide is the gate and broad is the road that leads to destruction, and many enter through it. But small is the gate and narrow the road that leads to life, and only a few find it" (Mt 7:13-14).

In the parallel passage in Luke 13, a listener asks Jesus if only a few will be saved. The context is interesting. At least this listener sensed this was Jesus' meaning. As Jesus responded, he used the metaphor of doors and gates. The door or gate is *narrow* leading to life. *Few find it*. This is a sobering truth. If it were the only time he spoke in this vein, it would be easy to dismiss. But there is more. Only two verses later he speaks of the same idea: "Every good tree bears good fruit, but a bad tree bears bad fruit. A good tree cannot bear bad fruit, and a bad tree cannot bear good fruit. Every tree that does not bear good fruit is cut down and thrown into the fire. Thus, by their fruit you will recognize them" (Mt 7:17-20).

For more on this notion, see several of the kingdom parables in Matthew 13:30-50. Look also at Matthew 7:21-27. These words and others suggest that belief in Christ—true saving faith—requires more than a quick prayer or immersion in a pool. We are not advocating works righteousness. We are disallowing "easy believism" as saving faith.

Contrasting these demands of faith is the equal reality of the overwhelming grace of God and his abiding love for the whole world. So great is this grace that many devoted believers can't imagine a loving God rejecting anyone. But it almost seems such theology rewrites Matthew 7 and Luke 13 to say, "The door and gate is wide, and many choose it." We wish the text and the comprehensive testimony of Jesus said this. I (Lon) believe that heaven will have fewer people from a broader constituency than I used to believe.

If one accepts that the way is narrower than we've imagined, we must never use this teaching as an excuse to become lazy or lax in helping inquirers come to saving faith that results in maturity. Jesus also said the poor would always be with us, but that doesn't mean we are to disregard them. Rather let us labor with all the more urgent diligence to feed the poor and fully assure the salvation of the seeking.

HIGHER CALIBER PRESERVATION

Can the church do a better job of preserving the harvest of hearts? Of course. When we use the term *church*, we include the ministry of the evangelist and his or her organization, as well as the ministries of local churches and parachurch organizations.

The evangelist must clearly represent the call of Christ in the proclamation. Be aware that in most societies, and especially in the West, the worldview promotes the pursuit of happiness as the highest of values. Make sure the gospel is not presented as an add-on to life, something to provide the next rung of happiness for the responder. Present the demands of the gospel primarily by emphasizing lordship concepts, even as you invite people to follow Christ. Emphasize the fuller biblical concept of being "in Christ," rather than Christ in you. Overall, we evangelists have done a poor job of presenting the reality of sin and its power and penalty, as well as the call to lordship. Let your listeners know from the beginning that committing to Christ will yield abundant life, but at the great cost of letting Christ take command. Present these truths with great passion, grace and longing. Persuade the listener that it is worth everything to find and surrender to Christ. (For more on this idea, reread chapter six, "The Lost Gospel.")

Once a person makes a faith decision, *urgent care* is required. Care goes without saying, but sometimes we forget the *urgent*. Satan seeks to steal the heart of this person and will immediately attack on numerous fronts. Time is of the essence. In a Graham mission, the evangelist starts the discipleship process before inquirers leave the stadium. He lovingly tells them of the importance of prayer, the Bible, a local church home and the need to share new faith with someone else. On the night of decision, a personal letter is sent to the home of the inquirer, welcoming him or her to God's family and reiterating things said in the stadium. The letter is addressed personally to the inquirer and includes the evangelist's signature.

A local church is given the inquirer's name for personal follow-up within three days. The counselor who prayed with the inquirer is encouraged to give a call. Graham staff stays in a city for a full two months, working with the church to make sure every inquirer receives spiritual care, if he or she is willing. Impact World Tour is considering leaving staff in a city for longer periods to work the preservation plan. That's how vital this is.

PRESERVATION REQUIRES RELATIONSHIPS

Emphasizing relationships more than religious events and even more than local church contact is important. When Jesus became flesh, God was stating the value of the gospel in flesh and blood. The very best person to help an inquirer is the one who invited or brought him or her to the event. In many Western countries with significant Christian populations, more than 80 percent of the people who make decisions for Christ are brought to the event by someone they know. Where possible, not only should the inquirer be invited to come forward or to stay after the meeting, but the inviter should be there as well. The inviter can participate in the first stages of discipleship. Make this reality a part of training your congregation or youth group before the proclamation event occurs. These inviters are the key to enfolding inquirers into community.

Where an existing relationship with a believer is missing, as it is in most places where there is little Christian influence or population, it is important that the first Christian persons to reach out to the inquirer are grace filled and truth driven. They need to be friendly and not put off by sinful lifestyles. They must also have the patience and perseverance of Job. Discipleship takes time and has bumps all over the place. The best atmosphere for early follow-up is either one-on-one or in a small group of other inquirers.

The seekers will have various perceptions of church people and church services, especially if they have little or no Christian background. Therefore provide a pre-church setting for them to begin their growth. Small groups are great in this regard. The leaders must not only be grace-filled and kind; they must also know the power of the Word and be committed to helping place it immediately in the lives of the inquirers. The Word is the true instructor in godliness.

In a sense, it is necessary to "cocoon" new inquirers to protect them from the world. It is also necessary at times to "cocoon" them from the church. We mean no disrespect. The church's unique language, music, governance and so on can be very foreboding to new people, especially to those who are completely unchurched. It is scary—like being in a different country. Therefore cocooning new believers for several weeks or a few months before guiding them into a local church may be helpful.

For local churches that want to host regular evangelistic events, make sure the follow-up leaders are ready and small groups are prepared in advance of the event. These groups should spend some time together getting the kinks out before seekers and new believers arrive. Many churches are using Alpha Course groups to provide the atmosphere and content for discipleship. Whether it is Alpha or one of many kinds of programs available, make sure the biblical content is relevant for a seeker or fresh believer. These groups are best led by those with gifts of evangelism and hospitality, or by teachers who are sensitive to early-stage believers.

As said above, local church services become vital to the new believer, but only after several weeks and sometimes months of individual and small group follow-up. Group leaders and Christian friends should be with the new believers at worship services for several weeks, introducing them to new believers and helping to explain the elements in Christian worship and practice. These friends are literally "translators."

Finally, in the earliest stages of discipleship, teach the principles of telling others about Christ. Nothing so nurtures one's faith as sharing it with others.

Perseverance is half of the work of evangelism. Let's quit arguing over who is to blame for our sad results. Let us pray diligently and get to work. The harvest awaits and our God is able to keep them from falling (see Jude 24).

EPILOGUE

FAITH AND VISION—WHO WILL HEAR AND BELIEVE?

The apostles changed their world by proclaiming and demonstrating Christ. Through their time spent with Jesus and their own ministry experience they learned the necessity of faith. Without vision, which is our hope, and corresponding faith, nothing happens. This epilogue tells two stories from our lives about God asking us to proclaim Christ publicly in settings requiring great faith. Mark's story is of an area-wide campaign. Lon's story surrounds the planting of a church for unchurched people.

MARK'S FAITH AND VISION STORY

I was just sitting down to dinner at home when the phone rang. On the other end was Jim Stier, international chairman of Youth With A Mission, calling from Brazil. He got right to the point: "Mark, why don't you do the Impact World Tour in Fortaleza, Brazil?"

"When?" I asked.

"May, of next year."

My mind immediately went to the overwhelming schedule of campaigns we had in front of us. It usually takes three to five years to find and train the necessary staff and build the infrastructure for a campaign. We were already understaffed working in more than seventy different cities on three continents. The idea of one more nation was absurd.

"Jim," I answered, "that sounds a little quick. It takes us years to get ready for a campaign. How big is Fortaleza anyway?"

"Two to two- and-a-half million," he responded.

"Two million! That's a big city. That would be a huge campaign with a large budget."

"A lot of the work has already been done by one of our missionaries," Jim assured me. "His name is Tony Lima. He's raising a budget of a million dollars, and the churches are on board with him. Would you at least pray about it?"

Knowing that was a question I couldn't refuse, I agreed: "Uh, yeah, sure, I'll pray about it."

After saying our goodbyes, I sat in the chair in my bedroom having a one-way conversation with God. I explained to him all the reasons we couldn't do a campaign in Fortaleza. "Lord, you know we don't have the staff; we don't have coordinators who speak Portuguese and it takes two years to set up a city of that size." Even while I was telling God these things, I had a sense in my heart that I was missing something.

A change of mind. October, November and December went by. Jim didn't call back, and I wasn't about to call him. I had convinced myself that the idea of the campaign was so impossible it wasn't even worth considering. As January rolled around, I did what I often do: pray and ask the Lord to show me what we were doing right in ministry and what needed to change. I asked Jason Gardiner, one of our coordinators, to join me during this prayer time. I told Jason about Jim's ridiculous suggestion, and he laughed with me.

Jason and I had been praying only about thirty minutes when we both got very quiet. The presence of the Lord was strong and serious. I said, "Jason, what are you getting from the Lord?"

He hesitated, then sheepishly answered, "I think we're missing God on this Brazil thing." I had gotten the same message. The next hour was filled with repentance and surrender to the plan of God for the city of Fortaleza.

Jason decided that he and his wife could go to Brazil and lead the campaign coordination. "Karen would love Brazil!" Jason said. "Let me call her." After a few minutes of conversation, Karen agreed to join Jason with their two children in the mission field.

The faith for the vision. A few weeks later, Jason and I boarded a plane for Brazil. We would meet with Tony, the local missionary, to see what was still needed. Little did we know what lay ahead.

As we walked out of the airplane terminal, we could see Tony's smiling face. For several years, Tony had been building and leading a YWAM base just outside the city.

"It's good to see you," Tony said while embracing Jason and me. Once in the car, I asked Tony, "Tell us, how are things going?"

Tony paused. "It hasn't gone as well as I had hoped. We are a little short on the budget."

"What's a little short?" I asked. "How much of the one million dollar budget have you raised"?

Tony looked down and replied, "Actually, none."

"None? What do you mean, none?"

"We had a plan, but it didn't work very well. We were going to sell T-shirts and videos, but they didn't sell like we thought."

"You must have sold some."

"We did, but the income went to pay for the office."

I could hear Jason groaning in the back seat of the car. In the hours that followed, we learned the rest of the story. Fortaleza, Brazil, was hosting a gathering of YWAM missionaries from all over the world, including the top leaders in our organization. When Tony heard that the conference was coming, he began to dream about evangelizing the city using these missionary leaders as speakers. After much prayer, he and his staff believed that God was showing them that one hundred thousand people would come to Christ in Fortaleza in the same year as the conference. Acting on this word, Tony began meeting with church leaders in the city, persuading them that a great move of God was coming.

But in the months prior to Jason's and my arrival, the vision had begun to die among the pastors. Only nine of the original seventy were still involved, and even they doubted what Tony said he had received from the Lord.

The role of steadfast faith. As we settled into our hotel the first night, Jason and I were filled with all kinds of emotions ranging from anger to confusion. We thought it best to pray. The first ten minutes of our prayer time was filled questions. "Lord, what do you want? Did you lead Tony? What do you want us to do?"

Then God's presence began to fill the room. We could both sense that God had a big plan for the city and for the nation of Brazil and that we were part of it. As we prayed, the anger was replaced with understanding of what God had shown Tony. God had indeed given Tony a vision to reach the city—because he was willing to be used by the Lord, not because he knew how.

At one point in our prayer time, I looked out of the window of our hotel room. Ten stories below, I could see young boys and girls standing on the corners waiting to be picked up by older men to be used as prostitutes. My heart broke. These ten- and eleven-year-olds were the same age as my own children. God reminded me that what we were doing was not about just big events, but about reaching these children and thousands like them, all lost and hurting.

At the end of our prayer time, the two of us knelt and recommitted ourselves to the task ahead of us. We went to sleep knowing we were in the will of God even though every circumstance was working against us.

Preparing for the campaign. The following days were filled with pastors' meetings, strategy sessions and physical preparations. We helped Tony redo his plans and bring the pastors back on board. Jason Gardiner, other staff, and all their families from the United States and Europe moved to Brazil immediately. Brazilian missionary Adernailton Sampiao (we just call him Ton) returned to Brazil to help Jason with the setup.

The staff began four months of fifteen-hour workdays. Christians from the city came seven days a week to pray. Eventually more than four thousand people were part of the prayer chain asking for an outpouring of God's Spirit in Fortaleza.

The gloomy atmosphere began to change. Churches all over the city became involved, and soon almost two hundred churches were working and praying. In all, almost ten thousand volunteers worked on eleven different committees. Jason oversaw 152 church fundraisers in just fifteen weeks. Old bills that Tony had accumulated were paid off, and the necessary campaign funds were now in the bank.

Before the campaign. The main evangelistic event would be held in the forty-thousand-seat football arena. Our evangelistic teams would also go into all the public schools, prisons and the cultural center, and they would minister to the military police. We believed God wanted to saturate the city with the gospel.

The weeks leading up to the main event in the arena were filled with evangelizing in the schools. Our evangelistic teams—GX Jam, Team Xtreme and Island Breeze—did as many programs as they could each day. Team members representing four continents came to help. This cross-cultural mix of people, along with citywide television advertising, made celebrities of our teams. The kids in the schools hung on their every word. More than 25,000 school kids surrendered their lives to Jesus in three weeks, and one superintendent called the campaign office to ask if he was too old to pray the prayer of surrender to Christ.

Island Breeze performed their cultural dance at the city cultural center before the city staff. Many of the staff gave their lives to Christ. Team Xtreme did a show and presented Jesus to 1,500 military police. The team leader, Kevin Stark, preached powerfully and more than two hundred soldiers responded, among them the general. After the general came forward, he walked up to the microphone and said, "I know what it means to be under authority. I have come forward to surrender myself to the supreme authority of all, and I believe many more of you need to do the same. It's time to stand up and come."

After he spoke, 400 more military police stood up and walked forward.

Ministry was going on all over the city. Thousands were coming to Christ before the main campaign even started. The move of God that Tony had seen in his prayer time months earlier was coming to pass.

The main event. The three-day stadium campaign began on Friday. Several hours before the program was to begin, the youth of the city were lined up in the streets waiting to get in. When the doors were opened, the entire forty-thousand-seat stadium filled in twenty minutes.

When I arrived there an hour before the program, the doors to the stadium were closed and thousands were outside hoping to get in. Jason met me as I came in the back entrance. "Mark, what are we going to do? The stadium is full and people are still arriving."

"They'll have to come to the second show at 8:30 p.m. Get the ushers together and tell them to go outside the arena and let people know."

During the first night, approximately sixty thousand people heard the gospel. At the altar call, our three thousand counselors were working with two and three people each. In the three weeks of outreach, almost thirty-eight thousand people had come to Christ.

Radio and television talk shows were filled with stories about our campaign. International Christian leaders who were there to attend the conferences were moved by what they were seeing in the city. For example, Luis Bush, international director of AD2000 and Beyond, said, "This is one of the greatest moves of God in our lifetime."

A true transformation had come to the city. Many of the youth who had just met Jesus were sharing their faith with others. The number of those coming to Christ was still growing, even after the campaign. Those trained as counselors were continuing to witness. Tony's dream, given to him by God, was coming to pass. Only eternity knows how many came to Christ that year, but Tony and others believe it was more than one hundred thousand—just as God had revealed in prayer.

LON'S FAITH AND VISION STORY

My faith and vision story took place twenty-five years ago. I was a happy youth pastor in a church in California. It was the midst of the Jesus Movement, and we rode the waves of God's Spirit for a few years. People came to Christ and stayed in Christ in astonishing numbers throughout the awakening. That's why I had no intention of leaving to do something else. After all, how much more exciting can ministry be than seeing nearly two hundred youth a week show up for Bible study at six in the morning.

The vision. It was my twenty-fourth or twenty-fifth birthday when a seasoned mentor, Jim Persson (about forty-five), took me out for pizza. While nibbling on the crust, he asked if I'd ever considered planting a church. "Nope," I said. "Never have, no desire." I rather liked my office in the lovely church on the hill and all those kids coming to and growing in Christ.

Jim took a different approach: "Lon, if someone wanted to start a church to reach unchurched adults, what would it look like?" This was fun. He wanted ideas but no commitment. Anyone could do that, and this was my world. You see, I had come from an unchurched background, and I loved the arts. I even worked for several years as a professional actor while also doing evangelism ministry. Our youth ministries specialized in connecting with unchurched kids and we were pretty successful, so I spouted off my ideas, including location (a nonchurch building—maybe a movie theater), music (contemporary, secular "with a point," and Christian), all the arts (drama, dance, media and puppets), Bible talks that connected with life ("communicating," not preaching), small groups to create community (rather than stuffy lectures in Sunday school). Drunk with the wonder of my ideas, I sat back sipping a Coke and finishing my pizza. That's when Jim dropped the bomb: "Lon, would you prayerfully consider starting such a church?" Ouch. Ouch. Ouch. "Okay, Jim, I'll pray about it."

I prayed for three weeks. A church for the unchurched began to sound good. It started taking over my thoughts. God was writing his will on my soul. Jim did more than pass on the vision; he brought himself to the task. With his position of denominational leadership, he had the clout to open doors. He and his wife became full partners in the venture.

A change of mind. As time went on, enthusiasm for the vision broke under the weight of reality. We had no people, no dollars, no building, not even a real wastebasket (I used a cardboard box in our rented office). Further, what was I doing trying to reach *adults*? At twenty-five, I still looked like a college student—and acted like one. The tempter was after me like he was, it seemed, after everyone else.

And the attacks began to come. Many in my existing church were aghast that we'd plant a new church within seven miles of the old one. Kids from the youth group were upset that I was leaving. Parents were mad. I still remember one of them taking me outside one day and telling me this venture was not of God and would fail. It hurt deeply that many older Christians who had helped form Christ in me couldn't support my new direction. Even though the mother church threw a going-away party, I knew many, if not most, were disappointed in me. The vision for a new church was blurry at best, and fading fast.

Steadfast faith. Again my mentor and colaborer in the venture gave me strength, this time over Chinese food. Somewhere between pot stickers and chow mein, Jim opened the Word and shared a verse he was clinging to in this venture: "Forget the former things; / do not dwell on the past. See, I am doing a new thing! / Now it springs up; do you not perceive it? / I am making a way in the desert and streams in the wasteland" (Is 43:18-19). Jim also faced opposition. He not only had local church members to contend with but also denominational leaders wondering whether a movie theater church with a twenty-five-year-old unproven, noncredentialed preacher could work. Unknown to me, he and his wife had also committed to borrow on their house to make sure I had a salary. We clung to that passage, and the Spirit's power on it held us in. We prayed, we fasted, we shared the vision with any willing to hear.

Slowly a nucleus of about ten to twelve people emerged. They were willing but not skilled in ministry. My parents were part of the core. So was a good friend from high school, who'd been soundly converted out of a life of drugs and sex. My fiancée, Marie, was there too. She had a special knack for caring for people others didn't see—the less popular and talented.

The launch. Our little ragtag band had a vision. God wanted us to begin a church for unchurched people. These were the early days of what we now call the "seeker church movement." Of course, at that time, the term *seeker* hadn't been coined. We didn't know of any other church trying to do what we were attempting. Ours would be a church geared to the marketplace of the late-twentieth-century California mindset. It would promote "change-able methods for the unchangeable message" of Jesus Christ.

First we found a movie theater. The only one willing to rent to us was an X-rated cinema palace. We had to clean up on Sunday morning after the movies (if you can call them that) ended on Saturday night. Broken beer bottles mixed with stale popcorn—and other things I can't mention—filled trash bags at the break of dawn each Sunday. Then a quick shower, change of clothes, and the cleanup team became ushers, actors, musicians and children's workers.

We opened on Sunday, January 15, 1978, to a torrential rainstorm. It rained eleven of the first thirteen Sundays. But God always gets the last laugh. As Martin Luther said, "The devil is, after all, God's devil." The X-rated movie theater became a plus. Why? The newspaper thought it was quite a story. The front-page headline read, "Now Playing—God, X-rated," or something like that.

We invited everyone we knew who didn't know Jesus. We even invited Christians to come once or twice to help us fill seats. After that, we were clear that this was a church for people without a church home. By church-growth standards, things happened. We averaged 350 by the end of year one, 500 by year two, 650 by year three, more than 800 by year four. At least half, if not more, were not "church-broke." But boy, were they broken. Disco dancers, a drug kingpin who made Christ his king, even Hells Angels came. College students and thoroughly unchurched youth found us and later brought their parents—and with them came their breaking marriages and addictions. On and on it went. We worked ourselves to the bone.

As we grew, we refined our "act." The arts got better. I really thought they were the drawing card. But no, it was Jesus and him preached. The preaching was simple (I didn't know any other way) but evidently clear. People found hope and healing. It is fair to say that hundreds, if not a thousand or more, met Christ in those four years. We made a ton of mistakes, as all new ventures do, not only professionally but in our personal lives. But we learned from them and changed course as God helped, forgave and led us.

We added leaders to disciple new believers, run the burgeoning children's program and the youth ministries, and help save crumbling marriages.

This church for the unchurched still meets in the theater (we ended up buying it), and it still reaches the lost. For twenty-five years it has faithfully presented Christ, and is even now entering its greatest hours. The pastors God has brought, the ministry teams, the lay leadership—it takes my breath away. This church is a vital mission station in a dark and needy land.

Vision, attack, faith, attack, sustaining faith, attack—we experienced these things and still do. But God is victorious over all. He wins the battles, he wins the war and we get to play with him along the way. As my kids would say, "Cool."

THE CYCLE OF FAITH

We've learned many lessons from our experiences. It would have been easy to stop when everything was going wrong. We could have said, "We tried, but it was just too hard." We could have blamed Satan for stopping us. But we didn't, and God prevailed.

There's a cycle of faith: First comes vision and corresponding faith by the Word of the Lord. Then, because of adverse circumstances, the vision dies. If it's to be reborn, the man or woman of faith must stand, even when it makes no sense.

Many people have dreams, and often these are God-given, but very few ever realize their fulfillment. Satan wants to steal the vision, to make it easier to quit than to go on. Yet birth, death and rebirth seem to be the biblical pattern, which is illustrated in the life of Abraham. Remember, God asked him to sacrifice his son of promise. And remember the parable of the sower: "The farmer sows the word" (Mk 4:14), but the seed doesn't always grow. Vision requires steadfast faith.

A fight follows God-given vision. In evangelism we are in a war for the hearts and minds of this generation. The war is real; the conflict can be intense. If we are willing to go to battle, to keep fighting even when things look tough, the victory is ours. If we stay in faith, we can influence cities and even nations.

APPENDIX 1

RATIONALE AND SUGGESTIONS FOR USING THE FIVE POINTS IN PRESENTING THE GOSPEL

The Reverend Mr. Dallas Anderson, Institute for Prison Ministries,
Billy Graham Center at Wheaton College

This small tool came out of a prisoner's response to me after a gospel presentation. He expressed his interest in the message, but could not figure out what the speaker was trying to say to him or what he was supposed to do. I realized that at times we are not very clear or logical in how we present the good news.

This was designed as a guide for gospel presentation to a group or individual. It can be easily adapted to meet your needs or style. The purpose is to help present a clear, concise picture of the gospel that is logical and understandable. Each point has a key truth that needs to be established in order to logically move forward.

1. God's Plan

Many people inside the walls of our prisons (as well as outside) do not accept the fact that God created the world in which we live. Yet studies show that most of them believe in a "higher power." They have been taught that our world evolved or began with a "big bang." Without getting into a debate on creation and evolution, we need to begin our discussion of the gospel with a statement of the reality that God created. If there is no intelligent Creator with a plan for our life, none of the rest will make much sense. The Creator created this world with a design to it. Life was meant to operate as he intended. We were created to live in relationship with him, as well as under his control. Too often I hear people talking about a plan that God has for people as if it is more about what they might do for God than about what

God has done for them. It may be that God has a special assignment for their lives or vocations, but our assignment is to let them know that his plan is that they might know him.

In our world, it is becoming increasingly important to start at the beginning. It builds a base for us to continue the rest of the story.

Key truth to establish: We have a Creator and he designed us with purpose and direction. We are responsible to him for how we live.

2. Our Rebellion Against That Plan

There is a desire within each of us to try to find some point of connection with those with whom we are sharing. At times I hear someone trying to convince inmates they have also done their share of "bad things." This may be true, but the point that needs to be made is not who has been "badder." In terms of the legal system, most of us cannot compete with an inmate in breaking the law (or getting caught). However, before God we all stand guilty of rebellion against his plan for our lives. We have wanted to do it our own way. We have wanted to live under our control. Be careful about trying to compare actions. The actions are really signs of our inner rebellion. We all stand equally before God as offenders in this realm.

At times we spend so much time concentrating on identifying the *fruit* of rebellion (individual sins) in our lives that we miss our drastic need to have our *tree* of rebellion cut down. That is why churchgoers often express how excited they are to have us go into prisons to bring the gospel to those who need it so much. Are we saying that we need it less? If we are, then we do not understand the tree of rebellion that grows in our own lives and separates us from God and his plan for us.

Sin always comes with a penalty: death. I like to tell inmates that we are all sitting on spiritual death row because of our rebellion and sin against a holy God. (By the way, unless you have stated that God created everything and designed it to be operated in a certain way and under certain laws, you are going to have a very difficult time communicating sin in our tolerant culture. If there is no truth from above, then everyone is free to do whatever is right in his or her own eyes.)

Key truth to establish: We have all rebelled against God's perfect plan. That rebellion is seen in our sin. Sin has resulted in our eternal separation from God.

3. God's Action

As we find ourselves separated from God, the good news is that God was not willing to leave us there. His love for us was too great to leave us without hope and a future. All of us need to hear how much God loves us and what it cost him to reconcile us out of our mess. He provided a perfect answer to our dilemma. That answer is the cross and resurrection.

We often hear people concentrate their whole presentation on the love of God, but let me remind you that the love of God only comes into focus when we see how truly unlovable we are in our sin and rebellion. What makes the good news good is that there is bad news for all who find themselves in sin and rebellion.

If there was no purpose for the death of Christ, then it is the greatest tragedy of all time. We know, of course, there was a purpose. The cross is a challenge to communicate in our culture. It has been beautified into a decoration or ornament and has lost much, if not all, of the meaning it had at the time Christ hung on it. Remember that death on the cross was reserved for the worst offenders. Furthermore Christ was innocent. He had been framed. And yet he allowed himself to be put on the cross. The Bible tells us he could have called ten thousand angels, but he didn't because of our problem and his love for us.

The cross is not the end of the story. He rose again! Here I like to emphasize that he not only died to forgive our sins, but he also came alive in complete victory over the evil one, and he lives today to supply all we need for life and godliness. The challenge is that he is present right now, right here and is asking each of our listeners, "What will you do with me?" They can try to pretend he is not alive, but there will come a day when everyone will see him in his glory. They have an opportunity to get their hearts right with him today.

Key truth to establish: Introduce them to the person of Jesus Christ. The cross and resurrection together form the foundation of our salvation. He died for us but is alive right now. The fact that he is alive forces us to respond in some manner.

4. Our Response

We need simply to lay out the steps of how people can respond to God's action. Confession is agreeing with God that we have sinned and rebelled against his plan and law. I am convinced that most people understand this even if they don't want to do it. Repentance is not as clear to most of us. To repent literally means "to turn away from." I describe that we are walking in one direction, and with God's help we come to the realization this is the wrong way and make a choice to turn 180 degrees to walk the other way.

Too often we do not emphasize that to come to Christ is to choose between your old way of doing things and his way. We sometimes give the impression that we can just add Christ to our life like a fire insurance policy and go on living like we lived before—almost as if we slip him into our back pocket and bring him out to apply to a situation, as we might need him. This concept is directly against all that the Scriptures teach. We must accept him into our lives as Lord and Savior. This is done through prayer and surrender. I use the term *surrender* more today than ever before. Our surrender should be presented as the only proper and positive thing for the creation to do before the Creator. God is in control, whether or not we admit that he loves us and has eternally positive plans for our lives.

Key truth to establish: He is alive and we have to decide how we are going to respond to him, whether we will confess and repent. We have to decide whose plans we are going to submit to.

5. Our Cost

I have heard the gospel presented many times over the years, and I hate to number the times I have heard it presented with no mention of cost to the recipient. It is absolutely true that salvation is a free gift. There is nothing we can do to earn it or deserve it. However, the very nature of the call to surrender is a call to abdicate control to someone else. It is to give up your rights. To give your life to Christ will, at the very minimum, cost you control of your life. That is what it means to submit to his lordship. It could very well cost us many more things, but it will surely cost us control. We are not presenting the whole story unless we also tell them this. Dietrich Bonhoeffer said, "When Christ calls a man he bids him come and die." It is only when we deny self that we can truly gain all he has for us.

Key truth to establish: The nature of surrender is to give up. We can't say we give up control and then plan to hold on to it as well. This is a call to a lifelong relationship in which we constantly surrender to his perfect plan for our lives. It is well worth it.

❖　❖　❖

Work with all you have to be as clear as you possibly can in this most important privilege and task of communicating the good news. Work to see if you can be even clearer next time. Our message is forever the same, but our audience is ever changing. Work to fine-tune your presentation of the good news as if it depends on you, and pray and trust, knowing that if the Lord doesn't draw them, they will never come. Salvation is always an act of God.

APPENDIX 2

AN OVERVIEW OF FOLLOW-UP

The Reverend Mr. Gary Cobb, Director of Counseling and Follow-Up, Billy Graham Evangelistic Association

The following is a summary of the steps in follow-up that occur in every Billy Graham Evangelistic Association (BGEA) festival and mission.

COUNSELOR FOLLOW-UP

All those who wish to counsel must attend a five-week training class, "The Christian Life and Witness Course." The initial focus is on personal spiritual renewal for the one who attends. The premise is, "Believers are not ready to share their faith until they are walking with God." The first two weeks are devoted to renewal. The final three weeks focus on counseling and follow-up of those who respond at the event.

Counselors are trained to deal with the most common spiritual commitments made at the events. Pastors and professional counselors deal with individuals who have deeper emotional problems. After the event, the counselors contact each person with whom they counseled to encourage them in Bible study, church attendance and small group participation. Counselors send a report to the campaign office that indicates the results of their contacts.

A colabor team is a group of up to three hundred volunteers who work each night after the service to input all of the inquirer information so that immediate follow-up can take place. They send a letter from Graham to each inquirer. The team also sends each individual's name to a church for follow-up. The goal is that the next day a church and the inquirer will receive information.

CHURCH FOLLOW-UP

Churches receive the name and contact information for each person who either named their church or was referred to their church. Pastors are strongly encouraged to contact each person and to send the campaign organizers a report of their efforts in a return envelope. As these reports are tracked electronically, those who do not respond concerning those referred to them will be contacted. If the church will not respond to inquiries, the referral will be sent to another church. We typically see a 95 percent response to our efforts in this area.

DISCOVERY GROUPS

In each city, thousands of people are trained to lead small group Bible studies for those who come forward. Many volunteer to lead a study for their church. These leaders' names are sent to their individual churches and pastors are encouraged to use them in follow-up.

Individuals who make decisions and are members of nonparticipating churches are invited to attend an independent Bible study in their neighborhood. Their pastor is notified about their decision and encouraged to follow up, but because their church was not trained, the organization offers the individual an opportunity for Bible study that may not be available in their church. This effort acts as a safety net to make sure no one slips through without follow-up.

LITERATURE

In addition to the *Living in Christ* Bible study given to each inquirer at the event, BGEA sends a copy of *Peace with God* and a subscription to *Decision* magazine. These are mailed a couple of weeks after the event. Once the inquirer completes the *Living in Christ* Bible study, he or she sends in a postcard and will receive *Day by Day with Billy Graham,* a daily devotional.

CD-ROM

The BGEA festivals and missions are now giving each inquirer a CD-ROM containing the entire text of the Bible, MP3 audio of the New Testament, seven follow-up messages, a video from Franklin and Billy Graham, and basic apologetic material to provide a biblical base for the new believer.

WEBSITE

In Graham's letter to inquirers, he encourages them to go online to the website. Inquirers can download Bible studies and follow-up material, or hyperlink to the BGEA Christian Guidance Department <www.bgea.org/ Biblestudy>.

TELEPHONE SURVEY

Two weeks after the event, surveyors call inquirers who made a first-time decision for Christ and inquirers who did not list a church. The caller checks to see if the person needs further counsel, if the person has been contacted by a church and if the person desires to be involved in a small group Bible study. The campaign office uses the results of this survey to verify that church follow-up is taking place. Churches are notified concerning any needs that are discovered from these calls.

NOTES

Chapter 1: The Power of Speech

[1]Adolf Hitler, Weimar Speech, November 6, 1938 <www.hitler.org/speeches/11-06-38>.

[2]Adolf Hitler, Munich Speech, February 24, 1941 <www.hitler.org/speeches/2-24-41>.

[3]Winston Churchill quoted in James Humes, *The Language of Leadership*, 60 min. Blackwell Corporation, 1991, videocassette.

[4]James Humes, *The Language of Leadership*, 60 min., Blackwell Corporation, 1991, videocassette.

[5]Aristotle *Rhetoric* 1.1, 1355.

[6]Mother Teresa, National Prayer Breakfast speech, February 5, 1994 <www.catholic education.org/articles/abortion>.

[7]Charles Colson, *How Now Shall We Live?* (Wheaton: Tyndale House, 1999), p. 17.

[8]A. Duane Litfin, *Public Speaking* (Grand Rapids: Baker, 1981), p. 18.

Chapter 3: Biblical Foundations of Public Proclamation

[1]William Arndt and F. Wilbur Gingrich, *A Greek Lexicon of the New Testament* (Chicago: University of Chicago Press, 1957), p. 432.

Chapter 4: The History of Public Proclamation

[1]Though numerous sources are used in this chapter, we thank Dr. John Akers for his brief but very helpful summary *The History of Evangelism in America*, published by the Billy Graham Center in Wheaton, Illinois. We are also indebted to David Larsen, whose "opus," *The Company of the Preachers*, and his fine work *The Evangelism Mandate* were of great assistance.

[2]Haddon Robinson, *Biblical Preaching* (Grand Rapids: Baker, 1980), p. 17.

[3]Rodney Stark, *The Rise of Christianity* (San Francisco: HarperCollins, 1997), pp. 8-10.

[4]Edward Gibbon, *The Decline and Fall of the Roman Empire* (J. B. Bury, 1909), 20:6.

[5]David Larsen, *The Company of the Preachers* (Grand Rapids: Kregel, 1988) p. 71.

[6]Origen, quoted in Larsen, *Company of Preachers*, p.73.

[7]Augustine, quoted in Larsen, *Company of Preachers*, p. 89.

[8]George G. Hunter III, *The Celtic Way of Evangelism* (Nashville: Abingdon, 2000), pp. 13-14, 63.

[9]Ibid., p. 23.

[10]Larsen, *Company of Preachers*, p. 110.

[11]Gregory the Great, quoted in Larsen, *Company of Preachers*, p. 101.

[12]Ibid.

[13]Martin Luther, quoted in Larsen, *Company of Preachers*, p.107.

[14]Larsen, *Company of Preachers*, p. 121.

[15]Francis Schaeffer, quoted in Larsen, *Company of Preachers*, p. 142.

[16]Luther, quoted in David Larsen, *The Evangelism Mandate* (Wheaton: Crossway, 1992), p. 62.

[17]Larsen, *Evangelism Mandate*, p. 62.

[18]Count Zinzendorf, quoted in Larsen, *Evangelism Mandate*, p. 63.

[19]John Akers, *The History of Evangelism in America* (Wheaton: Billy Graham Center, 1995), p. 5.

[20]Ibid., pp. 5-6.

[21]Cotton Mather, quoted in Akers, *History of Evangelism*, p. 7.

[22]Benjamin Franklin, quoted in Akers, *History of Evangelism*, p. 10.

[23]Akers, *History of Evangelism*, p. 13.

[24]Ibid., p. 19.

[25]Phoebe Palmer, *The Way of Holiness* (Wheaton: Billy Graham Center, 1995), p. 6.

[26]Catherine Booth, *Aggressive Christianity* (Wheaton: Billy Graham Center, 1993), p. 23.

[27]Aimee Semple McPherson, quoted in Edith L. Blumhofer, *Aimee Semple McPherson* (Grand Rapids: Eerdmans, 1993), p. 392.

[28]Ibid., p. 385.

[29]Akers, *History of Evangelism*, pp. 29-30.

[30]*Syracuse Post Standard*, January 19, 1900.

[31]Akers, *History of Evangelism*, p. 31.

[32]Stanley M. Burgess, Gary B. McGee and Patrick H. Alexander, *Dictionary of Pentecostal and Charismatic Movements* (Grand Rapids: Zondervan, 1988), pp. 655-56.

Chapter 5: The Case of the Missing Evangelist

[1]John Charles Pollock, *Billy Graham: The Authorized Biography* (New York: McGraw-Hill, 1966), p. 259.

Chapter 6: The Lost Gospel

[1]Sigmund Freud, quoted in Paul C. Vitz, *Psychology as Religion* (Grand Rapids: Eerdmans, 1977), p. 82.

Chapter 8: Seeking Relevance

[1]Helmut Thielicke, quoted in *Leadership Journal*, vol. 6, no. 1 (1985): 126.

[2]Ralph Waldo Emerson, Harvard Divinity School address, 1838, in *Preaching Journal*, July/August 1997, p. 6.

[3]Eugene Peterson, *Leap over a Wall: Early Spirituality for Everyday Christians* (New York: HarperCollins, 1997), pp. 3-4.

[4]Donald K. Smith, *Creating Understanding: A Handbook for Christian Communication Across Cultural Landscapes* (Grand Rapids: Zondervan, 1992), pp. 144, 161.

Chapter 11: Preservation

[1]C. S. Lewis, *Christianity and Culture, Christian Reflections* (Grand Rapids: Eerdmans, 1967), p. 33.